Bicycling

ESSENTIAL ROAD BIKE MAINTENANCE HANDBOOK

D1415944

TODD DOWNS
WITH **BRIAN FISKE**

Portions of this book were previously published in *The Bicycling Guide to Complete Bicycle Maintenance & Repair* (6th edition) by Todd Downs, copyright © 2010 by Rodale Inc.

© 2014 by Rodale Inc.

Rodale books may be purchased for business or promotional use or for special sales. For information, please write to: Special Markets Department, Rodale Inc., 733 Third Avenue, New York, NY 10017.

Bicycling is a registered trademark of Rodale Inc.

Printed in the United States of America

Rodale Inc. makes every effort to use acid-free ⊗, recycled paper ♻.

Book design by Chris Rhoads
Interior photos by Mitch Mandel and Thomas MacDonald/Rodale Images
Select product photography courtesy of the manufacturer
Interior illustrations © Beau Daniels/Artistic License Inc.

Library of Congress Cataloging-in-Publication Data
ISBN-13: 978-1-62336-166-2   paperback

Distributed to the trade by Macmillan
2   4   6   8   10   9   7   5   3   1   paperback

We inspire and enable people to improve their lives and the world around them.
rodalebooks.com

CONTENTS

PART 1 / FOUNDATION

PART 2 / CONTACT POINTS

PART 3 / CONTROLS

PART 4 / DRIVETRAIN

PART 5 / WHEELS

THE 7 RULES OF BIKE REPAIR

This book features core bike maintenance fundamentals that every road cyclist needs to know, pulled from *The Bicycling Guide to Complete Bicycle Maintenence and Repair* and packaged in a portable format. Before you dive into any repair, though, you should keep in the mind the following seven rules for any home mechanic. Keep a copy of this list in your toolbox.

1. Think safety first. Wear rubber gloves to protect your hands from solvents and grease. Use goggles to protect your eyes when using hammers or power tools. Watch where you put your hands in case a tool slips. And don't sprint away on a just-repaired bike—ease into it in case the problem isn't solved.

2. Don't wait. Small problems will eventually become severe. Preventive maintenance is the best way to take care of your bike.

3. "Righty, tighty; lefty, loosey." Most parts are turned to the right to tighten and to the left to loosen. The common exceptions to this rule are the left pedal and the right side of the bottom bracket.

4. Check that the threads match. Don't mismatch threaded parts. And never force things: Always grease threads first, then start threading them together carefully and gently.

5. Tighten gently. Bicycle components are often small and made of lightweight materials. Tighten, check the tightness, then tighten some more if needed. That's better than stripping threads and breaking parts.

6. Leave some repair jobs to the experts. Recognize your skills and limitations. Learn to make wise choices as to what you can handle and what's better left to a trained shop mechanic.

7. Have fun out there. There's no better way to get to know your bike—and build confidence in your ride—than to work on it yourself!

CHAPTER 1

FRAME

Caring for the heart and soul of your bike

Your frame does more than spotlight the bike's brand. Its material, geometry, and design help define the characteristics of the ride. Caring for a well-made frame isn't difficult, but it's good to know how the pieces work together—and what that means for you.

WHAT'S IN THIS SECTION

- FRAME BASICS
- FRAME CARE BASICS
- WHAT TO KNOW ABOUT FRAME GEOMETRY

Frame Basics

Anatomy of a Frame: Road Bikes

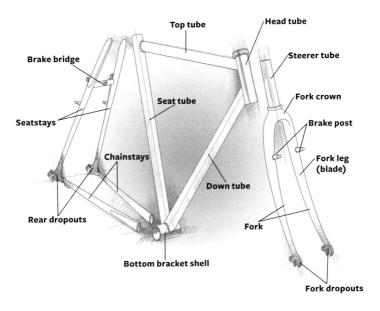

Top tube

Head tube

Brake bridge

Steerer tube

Seat tube

Fork crown

Seatstays

Brake post

Chainstays

Fork leg (blade)

Down tube

Rear dropouts

Fork

Bottom bracket shell

Fork dropouts

Frame Care Basics

Keep it clean. Salt and dirt can grind on frames and parts. Keep yours clean—but don't wash it with direct pressure from a hose, which can force dirt into your bike's bearings.

Keep it dry. You can (and should) ride your bike in the wet, but you should wipe off the moisture after your rides to keep corrosion at bay. Own a steel frame? Consider treating the inside of the frame with J.P. Weigle's Frame Saver spray (available online and at your local shop).

Watch the bends. If your frame is bent or misaligned, take it to your shop. Steel frames can be realigned; aluminum might be able to be realigned, depending on the bend. Carbon frames? Misalignment might mean bigger problems.

What to Know about Frame Geometry

Head tube angle: Steeper angles (up to 74 degrees on some road bikes) create quick handling; relaxed head angles (68 degrees or lower on some mountain bikes) make for stable descending.

Fork rake: This is determined by the amount that the front axle is offset from the centerline of the fork.

Note: Head tube angle, fork rake, and tire diameter combine to create what's called *trail*. To find trail, draw a straight line down the center of the head tube to the ground, then draw a line from the axle straight down to the ground. The difference is trail: Longer measurements mean more stability; shorter measurements mean quicker handling.

Seat tube angle: Steeper angles are good for high-cadence pedaling; relaxed angles are more for muscling big gears.

Chainstay length: Longer chainstays make for a stable ride; shorter chainstays make for more-responsive handling.

Bottom bracket drop: Draw a horizontal line from the center of the front axle to the center of the rear. *BB drop* is how far the center of the BB is from that line. More drop means more stability (noticeable in corners) but can impact ground clearance while pedaling.

CHAPTER 2

HEADSETS

Adjust and maintain this most-overlooked part

A properly adjusted headset can go years without needing much (if any) servicing, which is why most riders don't even think about their headsets—until something goes dramatically wrong. Here, we're going to show you how to keep a threadless headset running smoothly for a long, long time.

WHAT'S IN THIS SECTION

- HEADSET BASICS
- HEADSET TIPS AND TRICKS
- NOT SEALED? CHECK THE DIRECTION
- ADJUST A THREADLESS HEADSET
- TROUBLESHOOTING HEADSETS

Headset Basics

Anatomy of Threadless Headsets

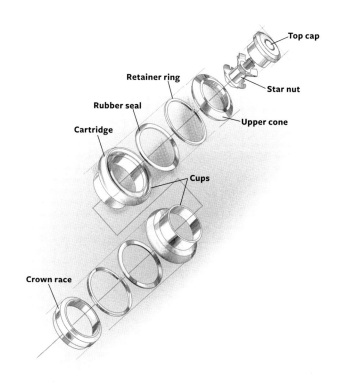

Top cap

Retainer ring

Star nut

Rubber seal

Upper cone

Cartridge

Cups

Crown race

Integrated Headsets

Instead of separate bearing cups that are pressed into the head tube, integrated headsets use cartridge bearings that fit directly into a specially designed head tube (see photo at left). These systems often rely on proprietary parts. Ask your dealer about parts availability, and check on compatibility before installing or the results could be disastrous.

Headset Tips and Tricks

When to adjust. If you hear a clunking sound from the front of your bike when you brake or go over rough ground; if the steering feels tight; or if the steering feels notched, like the steerer wants to pop into one position but not move out again—it's time for an adjustment.

Not Sealed? Check the Direction

When working with ball bearing headsets, be sure to install them in the correct direction (see photo at right). Each set of bearings has a top and a bottom and must be installed facing in the correct direction. If the retainer has a rim on the outside of the bearings, the rim should face away from the cup. Conversely, if the retainer's rim is inside the circle of bearings, it should nestle inside the freshly greased cup.

Check the bearings. If the bearing adjustment is always loose or tight no matter what you do, and you have a headset with loose ball bearings in it, check to make sure that you have the correct number of bearings in the upper and lower races. You may have left some out.

Check the retainer. If the headset feels tight no matter how you adjust it, and the bearings are in retainers, be sure that the retainer is properly oriented. If it's upside down, it will cause the headset to bind.

Buying new? A headset can be a good upgrade choice. The sealed cartridge bearing designs from Cane Creek, Chris King, Hope Technology, and others can last for the lifetime of your bike. We've even seen a few neglected King headsets that still perform flawlessly after nearly 20 years.

Check for bends. If the headset binds and you recently crashed, take the bike to a shop to see if something's bent. It could be that the headset or the fork's steerer (or the entire fork) needs to be replaced.

Keep track of parts. If you remove or are installing a new headset, don't lose any of the parts! There are several of them, and if you're missing one, there's no way your headset will work the way it's supposed to.

Adjust a Threadless Headset

Step 1

1. Feel for headset play by pushing and pulling on the fork with one hand while holding the down tube of the frame with your other hand. You can also lift the front end of the bike, drop it, and listen for a rattle. Another method is to apply the front brake and push and pull the bike back and forth, checking for a knocking sensation that would indicate play in the headset.

2. To check if the headset is too tight, pick up the front end of the bike and turn the wheel from side to side very slowly to see if you feel any binding in the bearing. It should turn smoothly; if it doesn't, it may be too tight.

Step 3

3. To adjust the headset, loosen the stem bolt(s), tighten the adjusting bolt (see photo at left) on top of the stem (or loosen it if the headset is too tight), and retighten the stem bolts to lock the adjustment in place. Then recheck the headset and fine-tune it as needed. If you can't get a good adjustment or the headset feels crunchy and full of dirt while you're turning it, you will need to overhaul the headset or replace the cartridge bearings.

Troubleshooting Headsets

4 COMMON PROBLEMS, SOLVED!

PROBLEM: When you disassemble the fork for overhaul, the fork crown race is loose on the base of the fork. (It should be tight enough that you cannot remove it by hand.)

SOLUTION: Replace it with a tight-fitting crown race, or try securing the one you have by applying a bit of thread adhesive to the crown and reseating the race. Or ask a shop to enlarge the crown race seat on the fork.

PROBLEM: You've removed the bolt on the top of your threadless headset, but you can't get the top cap out.

SOLUTION: You may not need to remove it. Try loosening and removing the stem—the cap should come off with it. Just keep track of the cap (it might fall off) and any cap parts that are inside the fork.

PROBLEM: You want to install a fork, but the fork's steerer tube is the wrong diameter for the headset and frame.

SOLUTION: It may be best to get the correct fork for the frame. If you absolutely insist on using a fork with a steerer too small for your frame, there are special headsets that can adapt a 1-inch fork to a $1\frac{1}{8}$-inch frame, or a $1\frac{1}{8}$-inch fork to a $1\frac{1}{4}$-inch frame. Because of the limited availability of $1\frac{1}{2}$-inch forks, there are several companies that manufacture adapters to reduce a $1\frac{1}{2}$-inch frame to a tapered or $1\frac{1}{8}$-inch size.

PROBLEM: You've loosened the stem bolts, but the stem won't budge.

SOLUTION: The stem may be corroded in place. Try carefully and securely clamping the fork crown in a vise and twisting the bar to break the stem free and wiggle it off. That didn't work? Apply some Liquid Wrench, wait overnight, and try again. Still stuck? Keep applying the penetrant and waiting, even if the process takes weeks.

CHAPTER 3

PEDALS

Give a hand to the part that connects to your feet

WHAT'S IN THIS SECTION
- PEDAL BASICS
- CLIPLESS PEDAL MAINTENANCE
- CARTRIDGE-TYPE SPINDLE SERVICE
- TROUBLESHOOTING PEDALS

Today's pedals come in many shapes and sizes, but they all serve the same purpose—to give your feet something to push against to turn the crankarms and propel you forward. Here's the basic info you need to service the most common pedal types.

Pedal Basics

Anatomy of a Clipless Pedal

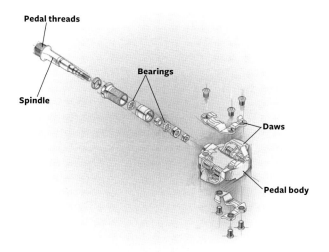

Pedal threads

Bearings

Spindle

Daws

Pedal body

Removing Pedals

The left pedal is reverse-threaded, so you must turn it clockwise to loosen it. Turn the right pedal counterclockwise to loosen. It can take a lot of force to remove pedals; protect your hands from things like the chainrings in case the wrench slips.

WATCH THIS FIX:

FIND A STEP-BY-STEP VIDEO OF PEDAL REMOVAL AT
www.bicycling.com/video/pedals-and

Adjust Your In and Out

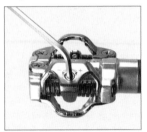

If clipping in or out of your clipless pedal is difficult, see if your pedal has a spring tension adjustment. Look for a single bolt on the front and back of the pedal (or just a rear one on single-sided pedals). Each screw will have an arrow showing which way to turn the screw to increase retention (usually described with a "+") or to ease entry and release ("–"). If cleat tension isn't the issue, check that the cleat engages the pedal completely and properly.

Clipless Pedal Maintenance

1. Know your maintenance points. The pivot points for the movable jaw parts should get a drop of chain lubricant every month or so—more often if they get wet.

2. Lubricating the cleats isn't always recommended, but pedals with steel cleats can get squeaky if they're ridden completely dry. A very light coating of chain oil on each of the points where the cleat and jaws make contact should be all you need. Keep it light—too much oil will trap dirt and accelerate the wear of the cleat.

When cleats wear, it becomes difficult to escape the pedals. At the first signs of unreliable release, replace the cleats. Before removing them, use a permanent marker to outline the cleats on the soles so you can quickly position the new ones.

If the cleat bolts won't budge, use a hammer and punch to drive the screws counterclockwise. Grease the bolts, align, and install the new cleats.

3. To remove the pedals, shift onto the large chainring, place the right pedal in the 3-o'clock position, attach the pedal wrench so it's nearly in line with the crankarm, and push down to loosen and remove the pedal (see photo). If it won't turn, ask a strong friend to help, try penetrating oil such as Liquid Wrench, or use a cheater bar on the wrench for added leverage (remember that the left pedal turns clockwise to loosen).

When both pedals are off, spin the spindles between your fingers. If they turn with resistance or feel dry, tight, loose, or rough, regrease the bearings. If you feel a smooth hydraulic resistance while turning the spindle, the grease is still fine.

4. Many of Shimano's pedals, as well as those of some other brands, come apart by unscrewing and removing the spindle and bearings as a unit. Use a pedal spindle tool or a wrench of the appropriate size to unscrew the spindle/bearing assembly. Hold the right pedal in a vise with the spindle upright, and turn the tool clockwise to unscrew the spindle. To unscrew the left pedal spindle, turn the tool counterclockwise.

Step 4

5. Some clipless pedals have a dust cap that you must remove to access the bearings. The cap can be pried out or may require the use of a hex key or flat-blade screwdriver. In most cases, it's relatively obvious how the cap is removed. With the number of different designs in current use, it's best to consult the owner's manual before delving too deeply.

6. If you add grease every few months, the pedals may never need new parts. For pedals with cartridge spindle/bearings, put about ½ ounce of grease inside the pedal body and reinstall the spindle assembly, which will regrease all the bearings (see photo). Lube Speedplay pedals by removing the tiny bolts in the ends and pumping grease in with a needle-nose grease gun. For Shimano pedals with a plastic dust cap, remove the cap and push grease onto the exposed bearings. Pull back the rubber seal on the spindle and push fresh grease onto the inside bearings.

Step 6

WATCH THIS FIX:

FIND A STEP-BY-STEP VIDEO ON ADJUSTING CLEAT TENSION AT
www.bicycling.com/video/adjusting-cleat-tension

Cartridge-Type Spindle Service

1. Remove your pedals from the crankarm, then turn the pedal spindles slowly in your fingers, and push them sideways to feel for play. If the spindles turn with a hydraulic smoothness and there is no play when you push and pull, the pedals don't need service. If the spindles turn roughly or you feel play, take the following steps to refurbish them.

You'll need a spindle removal tool for many pedals of this type (including Look, Mavic, and some Shimano models), as well as a bench vise to hold the tool as you

Step 1

turn the pedal body. If you have a strong grip, you can sometimes get away with holding the pedal in your hand and using a large adjustable wrench or 32-millimeter cone wrench to turn the tool.

Most Shimano pedals have 17-millimeter flats that most adjustable wrenches will fit. Be warned: These flats are soft aluminum, and an adjustable wrench is likely to mar them. If that doesn't bother you, go ahead. Otherwise, use Shimano's TL-PD77 tool or a good quality 17-millimeter cone wrench.

Step 2

2. For pedals that require a spline-fit tool, such as this Shimano model, clamp the tool in the bench vise with the spline socket facing upward, and fit the splines of the pedal into it.

Turn the pedal to unscrew and remove the spindle (see photo). If you look closely at the face of the tool, you'll see that it's marked to show which way to turn the tool for both the right and left pedals. Turn the pedal clockwise to loosen the right spindle and counterclockwise to remove the left.

Step 3

3. Don't force the tool. If it doesn't turn with a little pressure, you may be turning it the wrong way. If it doesn't turn, apply pressure in the other direction. After a few turns, you should be able to pull the spindle out of the pedal.

4. Clean off any dirt that's on the end of the spindle, which is where one of the bearing cartridges resides. Clean off any contaminated grease or dirt that you find on the rest of the spindle. Use a swab to wipe any dirt, contaminated grease, or water from inside the pedal body.

Step 4

Step 5

5. Place a dollop of grease on the end of the spindle assembly (see photo). Place a dollop about the size of a marble inside the pedal body. Turning it by hand only, screw the spindle into the pedal a few turns. Extract it and repeat. This will push the fresh grease into the spindle body and work it through the bearings.

6. To finish the job, install the tool on the spindle and thread the spindle back into the pedal body fully by hand (see photo).

Step 6

Sometimes the new grease will cause a hydraulic resistance that can damage plastic parts inside the pedal if you force the spindle. If the spindle resists at any point, extract it and start again. When you have hand-turned the spindle all the way into the pedal, use the wrench to hold the tool and tighten the spindle. Don't overtighten—it needs little effort to remain tight. The pedal spindle should now turn smoothly, without play. Rotate the spindle with your fingers to work the grease around inside, and wipe away any excess grease that forced its way out of the seal. Apply a light coating of grease to the spindle threads, wipe the threads in the crankarm clean, and reinstall the pedal.

Troubleshooting Pedals

13 COMMON PROBLEMS, SOLVED!

PROBLEM: A clipless pedal makes squeaking sounds when you're pedaling.
SOLUTION: Spray the cleats with Armor All or lube (just don't walk in the house in your now-oily shoes).

PROBLEM: The cleats won't engage when mountain biking in wet or cold weather.
SOLUTION: Spray canola cooking spray onto the cleats and pedals before a ride so mud and ice won't stick.

PROBLEM: You're having trouble getting out of your SPD-style clipless pedals.
SOLUTION: The cleats are probably worn so much that they can no longer spread the pedal jaws to release. Install new cleats.

PROBLEM: With each pedal stroke, you hear a click coming from one side.
SOLUTION: The pedal may have loosened. Tighten it.

PROBLEM: You're having trouble getting into clipless pedals.
SOLUTION: Make sure that the cleat is installed correctly on the shoe. Reread the directions or ask a shop for help. If they're Look-type plastic road cleats and you have small feet, you may have curved the cleat too much when tightening it to your

shoes. The cleats must be fairly flat to engage correctly. Shim the edges with plastic to flatten the cleat.

PROBLEM: Even though you're using a good pedal wrench, you just can't get the pedal off.
SOLUTION: Make sure you're turning the pedal the right way. The right pedal is turned counterclockwise to loosen it, but the left pedal is turned clockwise. It's still not coming off? Add a cheater bar to the pedal wrench. Still stuck? Try a penetrating oil such as Liquid Wrench, or use a longer cheater bar on your wrench for enhanced leverage.

PROBLEM: It's hard to get in and out of your clipless pedals.
SOLUTION: The parts that make up the jaws on top of the pedals may have come loose. Tighten the screws. No problem with the pedals? Check the cleats on the bottoms of your shoes. If they are worn or broken, replace them.

PROBLEM: You need to replace your clipless pedal cleats, but the bolt heads are full of crud or damaged.
SOLUTION: Clean them out with an awl, then force a hex key in by tapping on it with a hammer. If you can get the hex key to re-form the hole in the bolt, you should be able to loosen the screws.

PROBLEM: You installed the pedals on the wrong sides before you realized it. Now the left pedal is in the right crankarm and the right is in the left.
SOLUTION: Next time, look at the pedals right at the threaded portion of the spindle. Usually pedals are marked with an R or an L designating right or left. (The R pedal is for the right crankarm, and the L is for the left.) All you can do to fix pedals threaded into the wrong sides is to remove the pedals and hope for the best. Threading them into the wrong sides will usually destroy the threads in the crankarms. If that's the case, you'll need to replace the crankarms. Or, you can have a shop try to re-tap the crankarms with something called a helicoil kit, though this doesn't always work. The good news is that the pedals should be reusable, as crankarm threads are soft and shouldn't damage the pedal threads.

PROBLEM: Your clipless pedal cleats will not come off because the bolts are damaged or frozen.
SOLUTION: Apply a penetrating lubricant, then use a punch and hammer to loosen the screws. Use a pointed punch and strike the bolt to make a small divot. Put the point of the punch into the divot and strike the punch so that the force pushes the screw counterclockwise and loosens it.

PROBLEM: You stripped the threaded plate inside your shoe.
SOLUTION: In some shoes, it's possible to lift up the liner inside the shoe and replace the threaded insert. If not, it's usually possible to cut a hole in the shoe that's just large enough to allow you to perform surgery and replace the threaded insert. Then you can glue or tape the liner back in place or replace it with an after-market footbed.

PROBLEM: You need to remove the pedal but can't find a place to fit your pedal wrench.
SOLUTION: Look at the back of the crankarm to see if there is a hex-shaped hole in the pedal spindle. If so, get the appropriate 6- or 8-millimeter hex key and use it to loosen and remove the pedals.

PROBLEM: You crashed, and now it feels like the pedal wobbles when you're riding.
SOLUTION: You probably bent the pedal spindle when you crashed, which will cause a wobbly feeling when you're pedaling. This can also lead to ankle problems if you ride on it a lot. You might be able to get a replacement spindle, or you can replace that pedal or the set.

CHAPTER 4

SADDLE AND SEATPOST

Dialing in the height and position of a key contact point

The saddle is more than a place to park your behind; it lets you maneuver the bike with shifts in weight and should put you into the perfect pedaling position. Here's how to make sure yours is doing what it should.

WHAT'S IN THIS SECTION

Saddle and Seatpost Basics

Anatomy of a Saddle and Seatpost

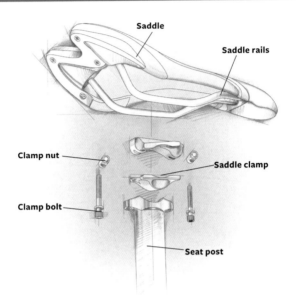

Saddle

Saddle rails

Clamp nut

Saddle clamp

Clamp bolt

Seat post

How to Position Your Saddle

Types of Saddle Clamps: Fine Adjustments Start Here

1. The tilt and fore-and-aft position of the saddle are controlled by the clamp that

Step 1

holds the saddle on the seatpost. Old-fashioned saddle clamps have a nut on each side that must be loosened before the saddle can be removed or have its angle or fore-and-aft position changed (see photo). The serrations on this type are coarse and do not allow for fine adjustments.

2. A second clamp type is the one-bolt clamping system, which allows for very fine adjustments. When this single bolt is loosened, the saddle can slide forward or backward, and the tilt of the clamp can be changed. The bolt is then retightened to hold the saddle in the new position.

Step 2

3. A third type is a micro-adjusting clamp, where there are two bolts working in opposition (see photo). Changing the tilt of the saddle involves loosening one bolt and tightening the other. This system allows minute changes to be made in saddle tilt and also holds the adjustment securely.

Step 3

Set Saddle Tilt

Loosen the seatpost clamp enough that the nose of the saddle can be easily moved up or down. Place a level or straightedge along the top of the saddle and adjust the saddle tilt until the seat is level (make sure the bike is on level ground to get an accurate measurement). Then retighten the clamp bolt.

Set Your Saddle Height

The correct saddle position depends on how your knees relate to the pedals at a particular point in the revolution of the crankset. The first step in finding this position is setting your saddle to the right height.

1. To determine the correct saddle height, sit on the bike while wearing riding clothes. Have a friend hold you and the bike upright, or place your bike in a doorway, near a wall, or in a stationary trainer that holds the bike level with the ground.

Rotate the crankarms to the 12-o'clock/6-o'clock position. Set your heel on the lower pedal. You should be able to place your heel comfortably on the pedal, and your leg should be fully extended—meaning it should be straight (see photo).

If there's a noticeable bend in your knee, your saddle is too low. If you have to rock your hips to reach the pedals when pedaling backward, the saddle is too high. In either case, adjust and retest the height.

2. To raise or lower the saddle, loosen the binder bolt at the top of the seat tube. Move the seatpost up or down as needed. Check to make sure that the saddle is aligned with the top tube and not turned to the right or left, then retighten the binder bolt.

3. Some city bikes and certain mountain bike models are equipped with quick-release binder bolts for rapid and frequent changes of saddle height. For most types of riding, however, once you've determined the ideal height for your saddle, it should be set there and left alone.

Step 4

4. When raising your saddle, look for the seatpost manufacturer's line indicating the maximum recommended height (see photo). It's dangerous to ride with the seatpost raised beyond that point—there may not be enough post within the seat tube to support your weight. If you can't set your saddle to the proper height without moving beyond that line, then you need to purchase a longer seatpost (or, possibly, a larger frame).

5. Any time you pull a metal seatpost (steel, aluminum, or titanium) out of a metal frame, clean it off and apply a fresh coat of grease (anti-seize compound or Ti-Prep is a better choice when titanium is involved) before sliding it back in (see photo). This protects the post from corrosion and makes it easier to raise and lower the saddle. Use assembly compound (a gritty paste) on carbon frames and seatposts (it can also be used if the frame or seatpost is made of steel, aluminum, or titanium). The grit in assembly compound helps resist slipping without marring the components. Never use grease on a carbon frame or seatpost.

Set Your Saddle's Fore-and-Aft Position

1. Sit on the bike (on level ground) with the crankarms at the 3-o'clock/9-o'clock position. Hold a plumb line (or a string with a weight tied on the end) next to the knee of your forward leg. Place the top of the string in the groove beside your kneecap and observe where the weight falls. It should touch your foot at a point in line with the pedal axle.

Step 1

If the weight falls in front of the pedal axle, the saddle needs to be moved back a bit. If it falls behind the axle, the saddle needs to go forward. Loosen the seatpost clamp, and move the saddle in the direction needed.

2. Once you've set the saddle height, tilt, and horizontal position, check the position of the handlebar. For general riding purposes, the top of the bar should be about 1 inch below the level of the top of the saddle.

As a rough guideline, check the distance between the bar and saddle by placing your elbow against the nose of the saddle and extending your forearm toward the

Step 2

handlebar. The tips of your fingers should fall about 1 inch short of the bar (see photo).

Racers may want the handlebar a little lower and farther away from the saddle; casual riders may want them a little higher and closer. If the distance doesn't fall within a suitable range for your type of riding, replace the stem to dial in your position.

WATCH THIS FIX:

FIND A STEP-BY-STEP VIDEO OF PROPER BIKE FIT AT
www.bicycling.com/video/make-your-bike-fit

Troubleshooting Saddles and Seatposts

7 COMMON PROBLEMS, SOLVED!

PROBLEM: Your seatpost won't budge no matter how much you yank, twist, and tug.
SOLUTION: Completely loosen the seatpost binder bolt in the frame. Apply penetrating oil to the top of the seat tube and tap the post with a plastic mallet to make it vibrate, which will help the oil penetrate into the frame. Do this every day for a week or so, and keep trying—the seatpost will come free if you wait long enough. If you're in a hurry, try this: Remove the saddle, flip the bike upside down, and clamp the top of the seatpost in a sturdy vise. Then grab the bike and rock it from side to side to break the post free. It's quite possible that some lightweight seatposts won't survive the process, so be sure you're willing to make that sacrifice for the sake of expediency.

PROBLEM: The saddle won't hold its position. It tilts up or down every time you hit a bump.
SOLUTION: The clamp is worn. Replace it. If it's a one-piece post, replace the parts that hold the saddle. Clamps usually wear out because the saddle loosens and you keep riding. Keep it tight and it should last.

PROBLEM: The seatpost is the right size, and the bolt in the frame works, but as you ride, the seatpost slides down in the frame.
SOLUTION: Remove the seatpost and lightly sand it to roughen the surface. You need to sand only the section of the post that will be inside the frame. Usually this will increase the frame's purchase on the post and keep it from slipping. Another option (and the only one if you have a carbon post): Coat the post with assembly paste.

PROBLEM: When you're lowering the seatpost, the post goes partway down, then stops.
SOLUTION: You may have bent the post. Remove it and lay it on a flat surface to check it. Replace it if it's bent. Not bent? Something inside the frame is preventing the seatpost from going lower, like the screw holding your water bottle cage. If the saddle must be lowered permanently, you can create the space to lower it by cutting a section off the end of the seatpost.

PROBLEM: The saddle creaks when you're riding.
SOLUTION: Drip a tiny amount of oil around the saddle rails where they enter the saddle and into the saddle clamp where it grips the rails. Leather saddles sometimes creak the same way that fine leather shoes can. There's not much you can do about this.

PROBLEM: When you tighten the seatpost binder bolt, the seatpost doesn't tighten in the frame.
SOLUTION: If you have a two-piece bolt that passes through the frame ears, it's likely that the bolt is bottomed against itself and can't tighten the seatpost. Fix this by adding a washer under one end of the bolt, which will allow you to tighten it a little bit more. This should then clamp the post in the frame.

PROBLEM: You've tried padded shorts and every saddle angle, but you still suffer numbness from riding.
SOLUTION: Try different saddles. Don't rule out unconventional ones, such as those that have strange shapes or cutouts. In the most difficult cases, you might consider a different type of bike, such as a recumbent.

CHAPTER 5

HANDLEBAR AND STEM

Care and maintenance of the second half of the bike-fit formula

WHAT'S IN THIS SECTION
- STEM AND HANDLEBAR BASICS
- REMOVE AND INSTALL A STEM
- ADJUST HANDLEBAR POSITION
- WRAP A ROAD HANDLEBAR
- TROUBLESHOOTING BARS AND STEMS

The handlebar and stem are the key to dialing in bike fit: The right setup can make your bike feel like it was custom-made for you (even if it wasn't). The wrong setup? Well, we'll keep that from happening with the advice that follows.

There are two main types of stem: threadless and quill. Quill stems are found on older bikes, and some hybrid and kids' bikes; the L-shaped stem slides into a threaded headset (identifiable by the locknut on the headset). In this section, we focus on the more common (and easier to install) threadless stems, which slide over the top of the fork's steerer tube and clamp in place.

Stem and Handlebar Basics

Anatomy of a Handlebar and Stem

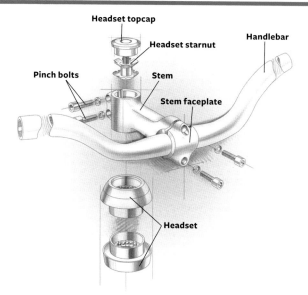

Remove and Install a Stem

1. Remove the stem's faceplate to remove the handlebar.

2. Loosen the pinch bolt(s) on the side(s) of the stem that clamp it onto the fork steerer tube. The bolts don't need to be removed, just loosened enough to release the stem's grip.

Secure the fork to the frame in some way. Run a shoelace or spare toe strap

Step 2

between the fork legs and over the down tube of the frame to secure it. Otherwise, once the stem is removed, the fork could drop out of the frame.

3. Remove the headset top cap. Most are held in place with a bolt that accepts a 5-millimeter hex key. Remove this bolt completely, and the cap should lift off.

If your headset uses a pressure plug (made up of several parts that jam inside the steerer, sometimes found on forks with carbon steerer tubes), use a 6-millimeter hex key to unthread the cap and remove it from the anchor in the steerer.

4. Remove the stem. It should slip easily off the steerer; if it gives you trouble, rotate it from side to side as you pull up.

Step 5

5. Reinstallation is a reversal of these steps. Fit the stem back onto the steerer and replace the top cap and bolt. After this, you can remove the toe strap or whatever you used to secure the fork in the frame while the stem was removed.

Tighten the top cap. This also adjusts the headset bearings. Hold the fork with one hand and the frame with the other, and push and pull to feel for play. Keep tightening the top bolt until there's no play in the headset and the fork turns smoothly from side to side.

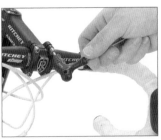
Step 7

6. When the adjustment feels right, center the stem and tighten the pinch bolt(s) on the stem's side(s).

7. Reinstall the handlebar, faceplate, and bolts. Set the handlebar angle to suit your taste, and tighten the bolts to fix it in position.

8. Double-check that your stem is properly aligned with the front wheel and your headset is properly adjusted. More detail on threadless headset adjustment can be found in Chapter 1.

WATCH THIS FIX:

FIND A STEP-BY-STEP VIDEO OF HOW TO RAISE AND LOWER A HANDLEBAR AT
www.bicycling.com/video/adjust-handlebar-height

Adjust Handlebar Position

Some people like to set their handlebar with the lower part of the drops parallel to the top tube. Others prefer to set the drops' ends along an imaginary line that runs from the top of the bar to the midpoint between the saddle and the rear axle. Set them somewhere within this range. To adjust the angle of the bar, loosen the binder bolt on the clamp (see photo). Rotate the bar into the desired position, and retighten the bolt.

Wrap a Road Handlebar

1. Clean off any residue from the old tape. Also, check the locations and tightness of the brake levers. The bolt for loosening and tightening the clamp is located either inside the body of the lever or beneath the rubber hood.

2. If the new tape didn't come with precut pieces, cut a piece of tape off the end of each roll that's just long enough to fit over the visible part of the brake lever clamp (see photo above). Set it aside until your wrapping reaches that point. You

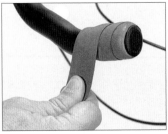

Step 3

can wrap two ways: top to bottom or bottom to top. We recommend the latter because the tape is less likely to unravel.

3. Start wrapping the handlebar at the end and work your way up. Tape the end of the tape onto the end of the bar so that about two-thirds of the width of the first tape wrap overlaps the bar end. Tuck the tape in, and push in the handlebar plug to keep the tape in place.

Overlap the beginning wrap completely, then continue along the straight section of the bar, overlapping between one-third and one-half the width of the tape. Keep tension on the tape as you wrap to make it stretch a little bit.

4. When wrapping the curved parts of the bar, make the overlap slightly greater on the inside of the curve so there are no gaps on the outside of the curve.

How to Wrap Around a Lever Clamp

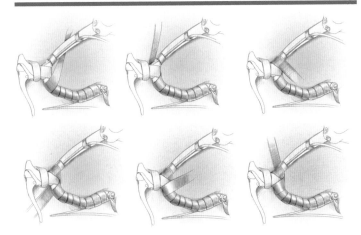

5. For a neat job at the lever clamp, wrap the short piece of tape around it and hold the piece there as you wrap over it in a figure-eight pattern (see photo).

When you finish making the figure eight, continue the regular taping pattern along the bar.

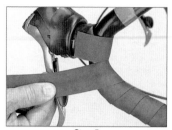

Step 5

6. When you reach the top of the bar, there should be a bit more tape than you need. Cut it to fit after checking that you didn't leave any gaps in your wrap job (if you did, unwrap and try again). Finish by wrapping electrical tape around the bar tape to keep it in place. Use a contrasting color to add a touch of class.

Step 6

If you wrapped from top to bottom, fold over the final loop of tape and push it into the end of the bar, along with any tape remaining on the roll. Secure the tape by pressing the plug into the end of the bar.

If you did not have enough tape to complete the job, you overlapped more than you should have. Unwrap most or all of the tape, winding it back into a roll as you go, and try again. Stretch the tape more this time so it'll go farther, but don't pull too hard on it or you risk tearing the tape.

WATCH THIS FIX:

FIND A STEP-BY-STEP VIDEO OF HOW TO WRAP A BAR AT
www.bicycling.com/video/how-wrap-handlebars

Troubleshooting Bars and Stems

TWO COMMON PROBLEMS, SOLVED!

PROBLEM: Your hands get numb while riding.
SOLUTION: Try thicker, softer, or differently shaped grips. On a drop bar, add padding to the bar tape. Wear padded gloves. Move your hands every few minutes while riding. Make sure the stem and bar position don't put too much of your weight on the handlebar.

PROBLEM: You tighten the handlebar-clamping bolts, but the drop bar won't get tight in the stem, and when you hit the brakes hard, they change position.
SOLUTION: The bar diameter and the handlebar-clamping diameter of the stem must match. If they do not, get parts that fit. If the sizes do match, loosen the clamp bolts, sand the bar's center section just enough to roughen it (on aluminum handlebars only; never sand carbon fiber), reinstall it, and tighten the bolt.

CHAPTER 6

SHIFTERS

Here's what you need to know about integrated braker/shifter levers.

WHAT'S IN THIS SECTION

- SHIFTER BASICS
- INTEGRATED BRAKE-SHIFT LEVER INSTALLATION
- SHIMANO DI2 INSTALLATION AND SETUP
- CAMPAGNOLO EPS INSTALLATION AND SETUP
- INSTALL TIPS FOR CAMPY EPS V2
- TROUBLESHOOTING SHIFTERS

Your shifters give you fingertip control for the gear changes that happen at the front and rear of your bike. This chapter covers the important setup and maintenance points for the most common types of shifters.

Shifter Basics

Anatomy of a Shifter

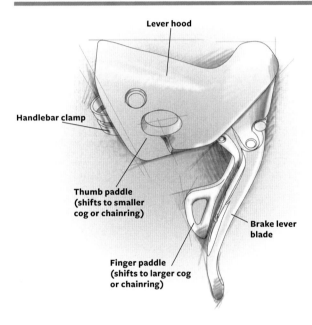

Lever hood

Handlebar clamp

Thumb paddle
(shifts to smaller
cog or chainring)

**Brake lever
blade**

Finger paddle
(shifts to larger cog
or chainring)

Know Your Brands:
Integrated brake-shift levers
produced by Campagnolo
(Ergopower), Shimano (STI),
and SRAM (DoubleTap) vary
slightly in how they work but
perform similarly: Shimano
shifters are made up of the
brake lever and a smaller

paddle underneath; twist the levers to move the chain to larger chainrings or cogs; push the smaller paddle to move to smaller rings or cogs. On Campagnolo shifters, a thumb-operated lever moves the chain to smaller rings or cogs. And with SRAM, one lever controls both the upward and the downward movement of the chain—push a little to move to smaller rings or cogs and a lot to move to bigger ones.

Integrated Brake–Shift Lever Installation

1. Locate the anchor nut for the shifter's mounting clamp under the brake hood. It can be found on the outside surface of the brake–shifter body on Shimano brake-shifters, and on the top surface of the body on SRAM and Campagnolo models. Loosen the nut so the shifter can slip onto the handlebar.

Position the lever on the handlebar so it fits your hand comfortably when you're "on the hoods" (seated and holding on to the lever bodies) and still able to reach the brake and shift levers from "the drops" (with your hands down in the curled portion of the handlebar). You may need to experiment with a few positions to find the one that works best for you. A good place to start is to install them with the tips of the levers even with the lower part of the drops; hold a straightedge along the bottom of the bar to line them up. Fine-tune your adjustments from here.

Once you've got it, tighten the clamp.

2. Now hook up the cables and housings. Shift the return levers until the cable spools are in the "normal" position—the point where all cable tension is released and the derailleurs are aligned with the smallest chainring or cog. For Campagnolo levers (left), push down on the buttons located on the inside faces of the brake lever

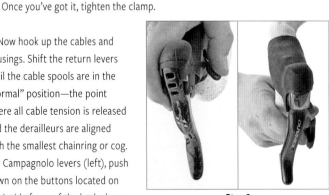

Step 2

bodies. For Shimano models (right), push the smaller levers (located behind the main levers) to the inside.

3. SRAM levers use a single lever blade that operates with a long or short push. A long push works the mechanism that pulls the cable. A short push allows the mechanism to release tension on the cable.

4. Squeeze the brake lever to find the brake cable access. Some Shimano models have a dust cover at the top of the brake lever that needs to be removed to get at the cable seat.

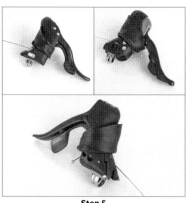

Step 5

5. Shift cables on both Shimano and Campagnolo shifters (top photos) are inserted on the underside of the rubber lever hoods. Access on SRAM levers (bottom) is on the inside surface of the main body. Roll the hood forward to find it.

Use new cables when installing shifters. Used cables can be especially tricky to feed into SRAM shifters, though with a little patience it can be done.

Push the shift cable into the opening until the tip exits the cable stop, and pull the end to thread it the rest of the way through. Sometimes gently bending a slight curve in the first $\frac{1}{4}$ inch of the cable will help it find its way through. Watch the cable head closely as it slips into the shifter body to ensure that it is going to land properly in its seat. A jammed cable head inside your shifter can be a real pain—at its worst, it can damage the mechanism.

Lift the rear wheel off the ground and turn the crank by hand to ensure the chain and derailleurs are positioned on the small-cog/small-chainring combination.

6. Run the cables through the housing sections and to the brake calipers and derailleurs. Be sure the housing sections have the appropriate ferrules (end caps) and are seated in the lever and frame stops.

Step 6

Make all the necessary adjustments to your brakes and derailleurs before moving on to wrapping the handlebar. Greater detail on adjusting your derailleurs can be found in Chapters 3, 9, and 13, and brakes are discussed later in this chapter.

7. Wrap the handlebar. Hold the brake and shift housings in place on the bar with a few pieces of electrical tape. The bar is most comfortable to grip if you run both housings along the front of the bar, though some handlebars have a second groove on the back to accommodate the shift housing in this position. Either way will work, so choose whichever one suits you. When the housings are in place, wrap the bar. (See page 29 for more detail on wrapping handlebars.)

WATCH THIS FIX:

FIND A STEP-BY-STEP VIDEO OF REPLACING SHIFT CABLES AT
www.bicycling.com/video/replace-derailleur-cables-and-housing

Shimano Di2
Installation and Setup

1. Since Shimano's Di2 designs are fully integrated systems, we'll go through the entire installation and setup for the shifters, derailleurs, and wiring in one comprehensive sequence, using Dura-Ace Di2 as an example.

Installation begins with only the crankset in place. See "Remove and Install a Shimano Two-Piece Crankset" on page 87 for details on this procedure.

2. The rear derailleur installs on the frame like any other. Thread it into the hanger with a 5-millimeter hex key.

Step 3

3. For the front derailleur, a small steel plate must be adhered to the frame on models that use a braze-on-type front derailleur tab. This plate protects the seat tube from pressure that's applied during an upshift.

If you're using a band clamp to mount the front derailleur, it's best to use a Shimano Di2-specific model. Other bands won't properly support the Di2 front derailleur. With this band, however, the addition of a seat tube protection plate is not necessary.

Step 4

4. The front derailleur should be positioned relative to the large chainring. A vertical gap of about 1 to 3 millimeters between the chainring teeth and the bottom of the outer cage plate (as it sweeps over the chainring) is ideal.

Step 5

5. With the front portion of the outer cage plate aligned directly over the large chainring, the rear portion should be angled about 0.5 to 1 millimeter inward (as seen from above).

6. Once you've set the front derailleur, use the support bolt to push the cage into position. Tighten this bolt until the outer cage plate is aligned with the large chainring. This preloads the support bolt so the derailleur can maintain its alignment during an upshift.

Step 6

7. Install the battery bracket and water bottle cage on the down tube. The dimension from the far end of the bracket to the nearest point on the bottle cage should be no less than 108 millimeters so the battery can be installed and removed.

Test the fit of the battery. Once you have the bracket positioned where you want it, fully tighten the bottle cage bolts and finish securing the bracket to the down tube with a zip tie. Remove the battery before wiring everything.

Step 7

8. The wiring connectors plug together; when properly engaged, the rubberized connectors are watertight and trouble-free.

Push the connectors for Junction A (with the indicator/reset controller) and

Step 8

Junction B (with the bottom bracket mount) together until you feel and hear a pop. Then inspect the connection closely, ensuring that there are no visible gaps in the seal.

Step 10

Step 11

9. Snap the terminals into the front and rear derailleurs. Double-check those seals. Any moisture that makes its way in may cause corrosion and impede the signal coming from the shifter.

10. Find a convenient spot to mount the indicator/reset controller. The best place is likely on the front brake cable housing where it's parallel to the head tube. (It should be within easy reach, both when you're on the bike and when it's on the repair stand.)

Once you've found the ideal position, fasten the controller with a pair of zip ties.

11. Next, install the connectors in the shifters; the one marked RD connects to the right shifter, and the one marked FD to the left. Rolling the rubber lever hood forward will reveal the connector bracket. The bracket on each shifter has two connector covers installed. Remove one of these plugs and push the wire connector into place using Shimano's TL-EW01 tool.

It doesn't matter which terminal you connect to; both are fully functional. The extra terminal is used for installing an additional remote shift switch if desired.

12. Reinstall the battery to power the system.

Actuate the shifters to test your electrical connections. If you need to remove a connector from a derailleur or shifter, use the flat end of the TL-EW01 to pry it free. Tugging and wiggling the connector out by hand can put unnecessary stress on the wire and connecting pins.

Once you've established that all your connections are good, shift the derailleurs into the large-chainring/small-cog positions.

When your derailleurs are properly positioned, disconnect the battery to prevent any accidental movement.

13. Temporarily fasten the wiring in place on the frame and handlebar with short pieces of tape. Make an S-shaped bend in the wire as it exits the shifter. Next, swing the handlebar left and right to be sure the wires won't bind or tug.

14. Hold the bottom bracket guide near the underside of the BB shell. The wire can then be wound in different configurations to take up slack.

Don't pull the wires fully taut. A small amount of slackness is better for the life of the wire, and it will be unnoticeable once the wire is fully secured with the wire covers.

When you have the cable lengths set to your liking, snap the cover in place and affix the guide to the bottom bracket shell with the bolt.

15. This diagram illustrates several of the configurations that Shimano recommends for winding the wire in the bottom bracket guide. It is possible to take in up to 120 millimeters of slack wire to keep

Step 14

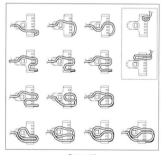

Step 15

your installation neat and tidy. Two more configurations (shown in the box) let you do the same for the wire that connects to the front and rear derailleurs.

16. Clean the frame with an alcohol wipe where the wire covers are to be installed, adhere the covers to the frame, and slip the wires inside.

Step 17

Step 18

17. Install the Shimano chain with the outer plates stamped *Shimano* facing outward.

Install the rear wheel and determine the proper chain length by fitting the chain on the large-chainring/small-cog combination. Thread it through the rear derailleur and pull the ends together. The length is correct when the rear derailleur pulleys and rear axle are all centered on a single vertical line.

Remove the necessary number of links from the inner-link end of the chain, and then connect the two ends using the special connecting pin supplied. Greater detail on chain installation can be found in Chapter 4.

18. Install the battery. Now you're ready to adjust the shifting.

Turn the crank and use the right-side shifter to move the chain to the fifth-smallest cog by pushing the full-shift switch four times.

19. Press and hold the button on the indicator/reset controller and release it when the red light comes on. You are now in adjustment mode.

In adjustment mode, from the derailleur's current position, there are 12 incremental steps in each direction to fine-tune the pulley alignment.

While turning the crank slowly, push the full-shift switch repeatedly just until the chain makes light contact with the next, larger cog and makes a little noise.

Step 19

20. Push the return-shift switch on the right-side shift lever four times. The derailleur guide pulley will now be properly centered under the cog you began your adjustment with.

Click the button once on the indicator/reset controller. When the red light turns off, you have exited adjustment mode.

Shift through the full gear range, front and rear, to test your adjustment.

Step 20

If there is any noise or hesitation, go back into adjustment mode and fine-tune.

21. Shift to the largest rear cog and adjust the low-limit screw with a #1 Phillips screwdriver. Back the screw out until there is a gap between the screw's end and its contact point on the derailleur link. Then turn the screw back in just until it makes contact with the link.

Shift to the smallest cog and repeat the same process to adjust the high-limit screw—but then back the screw out one full turn counterclockwise. This will allow a small amount of overshift when moving from the second-smallest cog to the smallest, ensuring a quicker, more positive shift into high gear.

Step 22

Step 23

22. Shift into the small-chainring/large-cog combination to adjust the rear derailleur's B-tension screw. Turn the crank backward slowly and adjust the B-tension until the teeth on the guide pulley are as close to the cog teeth as you can manage without them making contact or noise.

23. The limit screws on the front derailleur adjust like any other. Move the chain to the small-chainring/large-cog combination, and set the low-limit screw with a 2-millimeter hex key until there is a small gap (0.5 to 1 millimeter) between the chain and the derailleur's inner plate.

Shift to the large-chainring/small-cog combination and repeat the process for the derailleur's outside plate. Shoot for a gap of 0.5 to 1 millimeter here, as well.

Campagnolo EPS Installation and Setup

Note: We're using Campagnolo Record EPS V1 components in most of the examples here, but other Electronic Power Shift (EPS V1) systems are set up similarly. EPS V2, released in late 2013, uses many of the same setup procedures; the differences are noted in the text that follows.

1. Unlike Shimano's Di2 system, installation of EPS systems begins on a mostly bare bike, without a crankset in place. EPS is optimized for internal wiring; most modern road bikes have the necessary frame openings, but the system doesn't

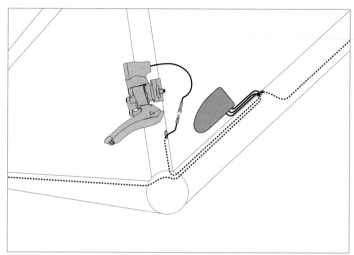

EPS battery placement

make accommodations for frames without them. Before you dive in, make sure the couplers on the EPS wires fit through the holes in your frame. Most important, with EPS V1, check the hole under the down-tube water bottle cage, where the wires attached to the Power Unit will enter the frame, as multiple couplers need to go through after other wires are already in place. If the hole isn't big enough, you might be able to enlarge it slightly with a small file, but check your frame owner's manual first; doing so could void your warranty.

EPS V2 battery placement (option 1)

With EPS V2, the Power Unit is installed inside the seat tube (the preferred option that we'll feature here), though other options include the down tube and under the chainstay. Internal installations require a small hole in the frame for mounting the battery charger connector; chainstay installations require mounts for the Power Unit bracket, plus a hole near the bottom of the bottom bracket shell for the Power Unit wiring. If your frame doesn't have these features, visit your local shop before making any changes. They can best advise you on your options.

2. The rear derailleur installs on the frame like any other. Thread it into the hanger with a T25 Torx key or a 5-millimeter hex key, depending on the derailleur.

3. If a band clamp is needed to mount the front derailleur, it's best to use a Campagnolo-specific model. Other bands won't properly support the EPS front derailleur. Attach the front derailleur to the band clamp or frame with the supplied hardware.

4. The front derailleur should be positioned relative to the large chainring. A vertical gap of about 1.5 to 3 millimeters between the tallest chainring teeth and the bottom of the outer cage plate (as it sweeps over the chainring) is ideal. The outer cage plate should be parallel to the chainrings. Once you find the position, tighten the derailleur in place.

Step 5

5. For EPS V1, install the Power Unit bracket. Hang the bracket on the water bottle–cage mounting boss on the down tube with one bolt (don't tighten it completely), letting the Power Unit hang to the side of the bike.

6. For EPS V2, the preferred installation is for the Power Unit to go inside the seat tube, wires first. Make it easy by using the internal installation tool (UT-PU010EPS)—basically a long rod with an end that threads into the top of the Power Unit. With the rod in place, hold the Unit against the frame with the rod aligned with the seat tube, and align the Power Unit screws with the holes for the bottle-cage bolts. Mark the location by putting a piece of tape on the rod that aligns with the top of the seat tube. Then, maneuver the wires into the seat tube, and lower the Power Unit into the seat tube (make sure you remove the shut-off magnet) until the piece of tape on the rod aligns with the top of the seat tube. The mounts for the Unit should align with the bottle-cage bolts. Tighten it in place with the supplied bolts and a 9-millimeter wrench. Install the shutoff position marker (it's a sticker) so that it lands above the bottle-cage bolts, and then wrap the shutoff magnet around the seat tube with the Campy logo above the position marker. Continue on your way with the installation!

7. Thread the control wires: Feed old brake cables or other stiff wires through the frame at the component wire ports—right chainstay, down tube near the head tube, and seat tube below the front derailleur mount. For EPS V1, these will exit at the down-tube port between the water bottle bosses; for V2, they should exit in the bottom bracket shell. You'll use these wires to pull the various wires of the EPS loom attached to the Power Unit to their correct locations. Using electrical tape, attach the EPS wires to the old

Step 6

Step 8

brake cables or stiff wires. The EPS wires are color coded to their respective components: green for the rear derailleur, yellow for the front derailleur, red for the Interface Unit, purple for the right-hand Ergopower lever, and blue for the left-hand Ergopower lever.

8. Pull the component wires through the frame, and connect them to their respective components. The wiring connectors plug together one way. There are arrows on both the male and the female sides of the connectors. When pushing the connectors together, make sure the arrows are lined up. When properly engaged, the connectors are watertight and trouble-free.

Install Tips for Campy EPS V2

1. Make sure the vibration-dampening o-ring is in position around the top of the Power Unit before installation.

2. The installation rod comes in two sections; note that the second section is reverse threaded—turn it to the left to tighten it in place.

3. With a seat-tube installation, most of the cables from the Power Unit will drop into place in the BB shell. The exception is the charger cable end, which will need to be gently pulled into the appropriate hole on your frame.

4. Note that the V2 Power Unit is compatible with V1 components, though you'll need a new Interface Unit and charger, along with the Power Unit, to make the change.

9. To connect the wires to the Ergopower levers, roll back the rubber hoods and remove the plastic doors on the insides of the levers. The color-coded wire connectors are inside. Attach the correct wires from the Interface Unit (which you've attached to your stem) to each Ergopower lever, and spool the extra wire inside each lever. Replace the covers.

10. Push the EPS wires and connectors into the frame, and install the supplied rubber grommets around the wires to keep water from entering the frame. Turn the handlebars to each side to check for binding. If there is binding, pull more of the wire that runs from the Power Unit to the Interface Unit out of the frame.

Step 10

With EPS V1, this is the time to wrap the wires from the Power Unit with the spiral wire protector and install the Power Unit bracket between the water bottle cage and the frame. Make sure the 5-millimeter plastic spacers are in place between the bracket and the frame. These will keep you from pinching the wires from the Power Unit.

11. Remove the magnetic pin, which disables the system, from the V1 Power Unit, or remove the magnetic strap from the seat tube if you're using the V2 unit. Now verify that the system has power. To do this, work with one Ergopower lever at a time, starting with the left side. Press the shift paddles on the left Ergopower lever to make sure the derailleur responds, then move to the right-hand Ergopower lever and repeat.

12. Temporarily fasten the wiring in place on the handlebar with short pieces of tape. Make an S-shaped bend in the wire as it exits the shifter. Next, swing the handlebar left and right to be sure the wires won't bind or tug between the Interface Unit and the frame.

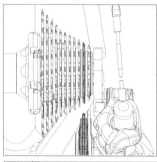

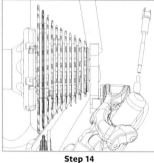

Step 14

13. Install the sleeve between the bottom bracket cups (this protects the wires from the rotating crank spindle), and then reinstall the bottom bracket and crank on the bike. Now you're ready to adjust the shifting.

14. First, you need to zero the rear derailleur. Situated just behind the thumb button on both Ergopower levers is a small round MODE button. Hold down both the left and the right buttons for 6 seconds until the blue LED on the Interface Unit lights up. This indicates that you have entered the setup procedure. Use the shift paddles on the right Ergopower lever to move the derailleur until the top pulley of the rear derailleur is centered under the second-smallest cog. Press either MODE button to save this setting—you'll know it's saved when the blue LED turns white.

Now use the shift paddles to move the rear derailleur until it is centered under the 10th cog. Press either MODE button to save this setting. The LED will now briefly flash blue to indicate that you have left the setup procedure for the rear derailleur.

Note about cassette cogs: Cog 1 is the smallest; cog 11 is the largest.

15. Install the Campagnolo chain following the manufacturer's directions. Install the rear wheel and determine the proper chain length by fitting the chain onto the large-chainring/small-cog combination. Thread it through the rear derailleur and pull the ends together. The length is correct when the rear derailleur pulleys and the rear axle are all centered on a single vertical line.

Remove the necessary number of links from the inner-link end of the chain, and connect it using the supplied Ultra Link connecting pin. Greater detail on chain installation can be found in Part 4: Drivetrain.

16. After installing the chain, shift the rear derailleur to the 11th cog and small chainring. Adjust the setscrew on the rear of the derailleur to prevent over-shifting the chain into the spokes of the rear wheel. Next, adjust the B-tension screw on the derailleur cage so the upper jockey wheel sits 5 to 7 millimeters below the largest cog.

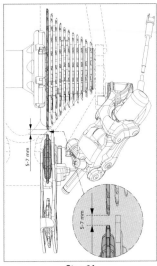

Step 16

17. Finally, zero the front derailleur. Press both MODE buttons again until the LED on the Interface Unit turns purple. This reenters the setup procedure. Use the shift paddles on the left Ergopower lever to adjust the inner cage plate until it is 0.5 millimeter from the chain. Make sure the chain is on the 11th (largest) cog of the cassette. Briefly press either MODE button. As with the rear derailleur, you'll know the setting is saved when the blue LED turns white. Briefly press either MODE button again—yes, without doing anything else. The white LED flashes blue to let you know you have exited the setup procedure.

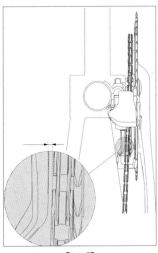

Step 17

18. Shift through all the cogs and both chainrings to check shifting accuracy. If the shifting is not perfect, keep reading. (Otherwise, you're ready to ride!)

19. To fine-tune the rear derailleur, first shift the chain to the second cog. Press the MODE button on the right Ergopower lever for 6 seconds to enter the setup procedure. The LED on the Interface Unit will turn purple. Use the shift paddles to fine-tune the position of the rear derailleur so it's centered under the cog. Each push of the paddles moves the rear derailleur approximately 0.2 millimeter. Exit the setup procedure by pushing the MODE button briefly.

20. To fine-tune the front derailleur with EPS V1, first shift the chain to the small chainring. Then enter the setup mode as previously described. Use the shift paddles on the left Ergopower lever to adjust the position of the front derailleur cage until it isn't rubbing the chain. Note that each press of the shift paddles in this setting moves the front derailleur approximately 0.1 millimeter. Briefly press the MODE button to exit the setup procedure.

21. With EPS V2, you can adjust shifting for each chainring independently. Shift to the ring you want to adjust, then press the MODE button until the LED on the Interface Unit turns purple. Use the shift paddles on the left Ergopower lever to adjust the position of the front derailleur cage as needed; note that each press of the shift paddles in this setting moves the front derailleur approximately 0.1 millimeter. Press the MODE button again to exit the adjustment setting for that chainring. Then shift to the other chainring and follow the same steps to adjust as needed.

When in the setup procedure, any inaction of 48 seconds on V1 and 90 seconds on V2 will cause the system to automatically exit setup and save the new settings. If these settings are incorrect, you will need to reenter setup and begin again.

Troubleshooting Shifters

6 COMMON PROBLEMS, SOLVED!

PROBLEM: After installing a new cable, the shift lever doesn't click the derailleur into gear like it should.
SOLUTION: Loosen the cable anchor bolt on the derailleur. Pedal by hand to shift the derailleur to the smallest cog or chainring, and make sure the shift lever is in its starting position. Then reattach the cable.

PROBLEM: A shift cable breaks while riding.
SOLUTION: Tie a knot in the remaining cable so it holds the bike in an easy gear and you can ride home. Or, if you have down-tube shift levers and a few inches of cable protruding past the derailleur anchor bolt, try this: Release the cable at the derailleur anchor bolt, push a little bit of the cable through the lever, tie a knot at the lever, and tighten the anchor. Voilà. You can shift again.

PROBLEM: The shift housings are rubbing against the frame and wearing out the paint.
SOLUTION: Put tape beneath the housings where they rub. Or, if possible, run the housings to the opposite stops and cross the cables beneath the frame tube.

PROBLEM: You move the shift lever, but the derailleur doesn't find the gear like it used to.
SOLUTION: Usually, you can fix this by turning the adjuster barrel on the lever or on the frame counterclockwise to add tension to the cable, making the derailleur move a little farther.

PROBLEM: It's gotten difficult to shift your twist shifters.
SOLUTION: Clean and lubricate the cables. Still hard to shift? Clean and lubricate the shifter.

PROBLEM: You're trying to remove a cable from a brake–shift lever, but you can't find the end of the cable.
SOLUTION: Shift the lever to its starting position by repeatedly pushing the return lever while pulling on the cable with your other hand (as many as 11 clicks might be needed to fully return the cable). That will expose the end of the cable.

CHAPTER 7

DISC BRAKES

Set up and maintain your hub-based stoppers

Some road bikes use brakes (actuated by a cable or hydraulics) that stop by squeezing a hub-mounted disc called a rotor. These brakes offer great power and control. In this chapter, we cover the setup and maintenance basics that will keep them working their best. For info on rim brakes, turn to page 62.

WHAT'S IN THIS SECTION
- DISC BRAKE BASICS
- DISC BRAKE MAINTENANCE
- DISC BRAKE CALIPER INSTALLATION AND SETUP
- TROUBLESHOOTING DISC BRAKES

Disc Brake Basics

Though disc brakes are more common on mountain bikes, they're becoming an increasingly popular choice on road bikes. Most road-oriented disc brakes today are a mechanical design, meaning they're actuated by a cable (much like traditional rim brakes). But the major component makers—Shimano, SRAM, and Campagnolo—either have a hydraulic brake in development, or already offer a hydraulic version.

Disc Brake Maintenance

1. Disc brakes work best when tiny particles of brake pad material are embedded in the surface of the rotor, so it's best not to clean them too often. However, disc brake pads are extremely sensitive to oil contamination: Even trace amounts of oil from your fingertips can affect your brakes' performance.

The best solution is to not touch the discs and to prevent oil splatter from reaching them. In the event of possible contamination, use a solvent that specifically states on the label that it is safe for cleaning brake rotors (many automotive disc brake cleaners will work). Many brake manufacturers recommend using rubbing alcohol.

Soak a corner of a clean rag with your chosen solvent, and wipe the entire disc. Then, with a clean, dry corner of the rag, wipe the disc again.

2. If oil gets on your disc brake pads, you may be able to salvage them by rubbing them lightly across a piece of sandpaper or emery cloth laid out on a flat surface. If the pads have gotten soaked with oil, or if heat is applied after the pads became contaminated (such as by applying the brakes while riding), you'll likely have to replace them.

Step 2

3. Disc brake calipers must be properly aligned. If you're sure that yours are properly aligned but the brakes still feel vague and mushy, the brake bosses may need to be milled.

Milling is the process of shaving material from the disc brake tabs on your frame to make the mounting surfaces perfectly parallel to the rotor. The tools needed to perform this task are expensive—this is a job for your local shop.

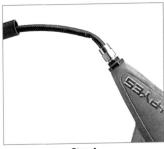

Step 4

4. A kinked hydraulic line is more than an eyesore. It can also have a compromised inner lining, making a brake failure likely.

If the line is kinked near a fitting and there is sufficient extra line, trim away the affected portion of the line and bleed the system. If the kink is too far from a fitting to do this, there is no choice but to replace the line.

Step 5

5. Rotors can, and do, get bent—particularly by rocks, logs, and other technical-trail obstacles. If yours is tweaked, remove the caliper, zip a plastic cable tie around the fork leg or seatstay, and snip the cable tie's end short to create a makeshift truing caliper. Use the caliper to gauge how much the rotor needs to be trued. Use a set of Morningstar disc truing tools or an adjustable wrench to straighten the disc. It may never be perfect again, but it can be made passable.

WATCH THIS FIX:

FIND A STEP-BY-STEP VIDEO OF HOW TO TRUE A DISC ROTOR AT
www.bicycling.com/video/adjust-and-true-disc-brakes#/

FIND A STEP-BY-STEP VIDEO OF HOW TO REPLACE A DISC BRAKE PAD AT
www.bicycling.com/video/replacing-brake-pads-disc-brakes#/

Disc Brake Caliper Installation and Setup

1. Most mechanical and hydraulic disc brakes are installed in a similar fashion. One noticeable difference is that many Avid disc brake calipers are mounted using a set of hemispherical washers. This ingenious mounting system allows the caliper to be aligned in all directions, compensating for inconsistencies in a frame's or fork's brake mounting tabs. The sequencing of the washers is critical to the func-

Step 1

tion of the Tri-Align Caliper Positioning System, so don't remove the caliper from the adapter (most brakes come with an adapter to position them properly with the rotor) until you have taken note of the placement of the hemispherical washers.

Use a 5-millimeter hex key to tighten the two bolts holding the adapter to the frame's or fork's mounting tabs; then use the hex key to loosen by about half a turn the two bolts holding the caliper to the adapter. The caliper should float freely from side to side. If needed, disengage the hydraulic line from its guide on the chainstay to help the caliper move more freely.

2. Avid mechanical calipers have a red dial adjuster for each brake pad; other mechanical systems use a hex key for adjustment. Turning a dial or hex head clock-

Step 2

wise moves the pad closer to the disc; counterclockwise moves it away from the disc. Use these adjustments to clamp the disc between the pads, roughly in the center of the caliper body.

For hydraulic brakes, wrap a rubber band over the brake lever and grip to clamp the disc between the brake pads.

Step 3

3. In small increments—a little on one, then the other—tighten the bolts holding the caliper to the adapter. Watch the caliper closely as you're doing this, making certain that it doesn't try to "walk" side to side from friction with the bolt.

Release the rubber band on hydraulic models. On mechanical versions, turn the outside dial adjuster counterclockwise, moving the mobile brake pad as far from the disc as it will go. Turn the inside dial adjuster just a few clicks counterclockwise. Push the caliper's lever arm by hand to ensure that the pad is pushed back, and give the wheel a spin. If there is any rubbing, turn the inside adjuster counterclockwise and repeat until there is no contact. There should be a gap of less than 0.5 millimeter between the fixed pad and the disc on mechanical calipers. Hydraulic calipers should have equal gaps between each pad and the disc.

4. At this point, installation of a hydraulic caliper is complete. Mechanical calipers require a few more steps.

Turn the outside dial adjuster clockwise a few clicks at a time, and push the lever arm by hand until it stops at a point about halfway through its travel to the cable stop. Anchor the cable in place using a 5-millimeter hex key. Use a cable puller or stretcher to simultaneously pull the cable and push the caliper's lever arm about one-quarter of the way through its travel. Give the brake lever a few firm squeezes to settle the housing and pads into place, then repeat your cable adjustment. In your shop, you'll find it's best to make fine adjustments to the lever feel at the cable anchor, rather than using the adjusting barrel on the lever. The barrel adjuster is there primarily to quickly adjust for pad wear while out on the road or trail.

5. Cut the free end of the cable no more than 20 millimeters, or $3/4$ inch, from the cable anchor. Any longer than that and the end of the cable could swing into the disc, locking up your wheel and sending you flying. Crimp the cable end to prevent fraying.

Step 5

WATCH THIS FIX:

FIND A STEP-BY-STEP VIDEO OF ALIGNING DISC BRAKE CALIPERS AT
www.bicycling.com/video/adjusting-disc-brake-calipers

Troubleshooting Disc Brakes

4 COMMON PROBLEMS, SOLVED!

PROBLEM: The pads constantly rub on the rotors.
SOLUTION: There are two possible solutions. Check the rotor where it enters and exits the caliper. If the caliper body is centered over the rotor, then you have a sticky piston (if it isn't centered, skip to the next paragraph). Remove the wheel

and brake pads. Hold a broad, flat tool like a bladed screwdriver between the pistons, and give the brake lever a few pumps to expose about $3/16$ inch of both pistons. This allows oil from inside the caliper to lubricate the O-rings. Spray the exposed parts of the pistons with rubbing alcohol to clean them; then let them dry. Use the screwdriver to carefully push the pistons back into the caliper. Do not notch the pistons—especially on their sides. Use firm, even pressure, and don't pry or twist.

If the caliper body is not centered over the rotor, or if the technique described above didn't help, repeat the alignment steps detailed in this chapter.

If the rubbing is an intermittent tick, your rotor may be bent. Though it's nearly impossible to get a bent rotor perfectly straight again, you can get it pretty close using a few common items. Remove the caliper from the frame or fork. Zip a plastic cable tie around the fork leg or seatstay, and snip it short. Now you have a makeshift caliper to gauge where the rotor is bent. Slide it into place so there is a small gap between the end of the tie and the rotor, and slowly turn the wheel. Using an adjustable wrench, gently bend the rotor wherever it deviates from true.

PROBLEM: Your brakes honk.
SOLUTION: Some disc brakes make noise; it's the unfortunate truth. Still, there are a few things you can do to mitigate the annoyance.

1. **Scuff your brake pads** (remove them first) on a piece of sandpaper laid out on a flat surface. You don't need to dig into the pads; a few light strokes will remove glaze from the pads' surface.

2. **Experiment with different types of brake pads.** Different brake pad compounds and even different manufacturers' interpretations of the same compound can make a big difference in how much vibration is created. Be aware that different pads will perform differently. Weigh the costs and benefits of ideal performance and low noise when making your final decision.

3. **Try a self-cleaning "wave" disc.** A wave-shaped disc will gently scrape the brake pads clean with each pass. Some also speculate that the wave shape pumps cool air through the pads, keeping the system from overheating during prolonged braking.

PROBLEM: The brake line is kinked.
SOLUTION: There's no quick fix, but a kink in the line can restrict the flow of fluid to the caliper or, worse, develop into a leak. Get this fixed immediately. If the kink is

near the fitting at either end and there is sufficient extra hose to do so, it's possible to trim off the kink and reconnect the line. This will require some new fittings and a brake bleed. If the kink is farther down the line or the hose is too short to trim, replace the whole line.

PROBLEM: The brakes feel vague or mushy.

SOLUTION: If the brake lever pulls all or most of the way to the grip, there are a few possible causes.

1. **Check your brake pads.** If they're less than 0.5 millimeter thick, it's time to replace them. With new pads in place, the slave pistons will be pushed back into their cylinders, returning fluid to the master and renewing brake feel.

2. **Top off the reservoir.** If your brakes have an external reservoir, you can add fluid to the reservoir without performing a full bleed. Wrap a clean rag around the lever body, leaving the cap exposed so it can be removed. Take the cap off and fill the reservoir about halfway. Give the brake lever a few slow, steady pumps to evacuate any air and draw fluid down into the system. Lightly tap the lever body to help air escape. When there's no more evidence of air, top off the reservoir and replace the cap.

CHAPTER 8

RIM BRAKES

Set up and maintain your rim-squeezing stoppers

WHAT'S IN THIS SECTION

- RIM BRAKE BASICS
- INSTALLING LEVERS
  * Aero (aka Integrated Brake–Shift) Lever and Cable Installation
- INSTALLING AND ADJUSTING CALIPERS
  * Sidepull Brake Removal and Installation
  * Cantilever Installation and Adjustment
- BRAKE HELP
  * Brake Pad Maintenance
- TROUBLESHOOTING RIM BRAKES

Brakes come in many shapes and sizes; most road bikes use stoppers that squeeze the rims to bring your forward motion to a halt. In this section, we cover the basics of setup and maintenance for the most common types of rim brakes. For info on disc brakes, turn to page 54.

Rim Brake Basics

Anatomy of a Road Bike Rim Brake

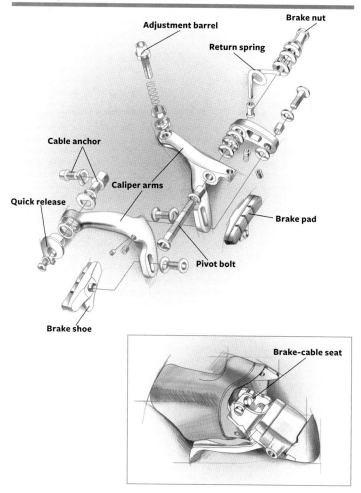

Adjustment barrel

Brake nut

Return spring

Cable anchor

Caliper arms

Quick release

Brake pad

Pivot bolt

Brake shoe

Brake-cable seat

Cable-Housing Care

Cut cable housing with a sharp pair of cable or diagonal cutters. If a burr forms at the end, snip it away. File the end of the housing flat so that it doesn't try to bite in under pressure and bind the cable.

Clean Rims Mean Better Braking

The road grime that builds up on your rims can interfere with good braking performance. Periodically, wash rims with soapy water. To break up any remaining residue, use a solvent such as rubbing alcohol and fine steel wool or an abrasive pad made of material that won't scratch metal.

Installing Levers

Aero (aka Integrated Brake–Shift) Lever and Cable Installation

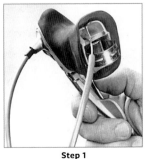

Step 1

1. When installing aero levers, it's important to seat the housing and ferrule (if there is one) carefully inside the lever. If either is not secure, the cable can bind and reduce the brake's effectiveness. With the brake lever off the handlebar, grease the cable lightly and thread it through the lever, ferrule, and housing (see photo). The cable end should be cut cleanly and travel smoothly through the housing. If it doesn't, recut the cable with cutters made for the purpose (such as the Park Tool CN-10 cable cutter). Make sure both ends of the housing are free of burrs; recut the ends if necessary.

2. Thread the brake cable through the brake caliper's adjustment barrel and anchor bolt. Use a cable stretcher or toe strap, or squeeze the caliper and pull on the brake cable until the head of the cable and the housing are seated inside the lever. Tighten the anchor bolt. Release the caliper so the brake spring tension holds the housing and ferrule in place inside the lever.

Step 2

3. Move the housing to the slot for it inside the lever, and wiggle the lever onto the handlebar. Roll back the rubber hood to make it easier. Tighten the lever in place. To position the levers, hold a straightedge against the underside of the handlebar and slide the lever so its tip rests on the straightedge. The lever should also face directly forward, not point off at an angle. Secure the levers by tightening the bolt inside the lever body with a hex key.

4. Aero lever cable housing works best when the rear section travels in front of the stem before returning to the top-tube cable stop. This loop provides enough slack to turn the handlebar without binding. The front brake housing should go through this loop to the front brake (see photo). The cable routing should follow smooth, gradual bends for optimal braking action.

5. Use electrical tape to affix the housing to the underside of the handlebar. Trim excess housing so the brake is as responsive as possible. To do this, loosen the cable anchor bolt to release the brake cable, grasp the head of the cable inside the brake lever with needle-

Step 4

nose pliers, and pull the cable out of the housing enough that you can cut off a section without cutting the cable. Again, make sure there are no burrs at the end of the housing. Use cable cutters or a file to fix this if necessary. Be careful not to cut off too much housing, which would cause the brakes or handlebar to bind.

6. Push the cable back through the housing and the brake anchor bolt. Use a third-hand tool to compress the brake caliper and pull on the end of the cable while you tighten the anchor bolt. Wrap the bar with handlebar tape (see page 29 for instructions).

WATCH THIS FIX:

FIND A STEP-BY-STEP VIDEO OF HOW TO REPLACE BRAKE CABLES AND HOUSING AT
www.bicycling.com/video/replace-brake-cables-and-housing

Installing and Adjusting Calipers

Sidepull Brake Removal and Installation

1. Loosen the cable anchor bolt and free the end of the cable. Loosen and remove

Step 1

the nut on the rear of the mounting bolt that runs through the brake body.

Thread the nut off the end of the bolt, then pull the brake body away from the frame (see photo). If you have removed the brake to service it rather than replace it, clean it thoroughly. Use a rag dipped in solvent, and a brush to loosen the grease and dirt that's on the surface of the calipers and hiding inside the nooks and crannies.

2. Unless you're using something mild like alcohol, keep the solvent away from the brake pads. Better yet, remove the brake shoes to clean the pads separately.

Since oil and grease have a tendency to attract dirt, use them only where needed. On sidepull brakes, that means only at the pivot points and the spring anchors on the back of the calipers.

To minimize the possibility of getting lubricant on your brake pads, use grease rather than oil on the spring where it rubs against its anchors. Because it is difficult to work grease into the pivot area without dismantling the brake, spray those points with a small amount of lubricant containing Teflon.

3. To install a brake, insert the mounting bolt through the hole in the frame, and thread on the mounting nut. Leave the nut loose enough for the brake to be centered over the wheel by hand. Reconnect the brake cable to the brake calipers, and adjust the cable length by leaving the housing loops large enough to enter the housing stops in a straight line, but not too long either (too long causes excess drag; too short can kink the housing). See page 64 for advice on trimming housing. Check the caliper alignment. (Make sure the wheel is true and centered in the frame before aligning the calipers. If the wheel is out of true, no amount of brake adjustment will give you good performance.)

Before attempting to center the brake, check the relationship of the caliper arms to each other. If they're too tight, they will not spring back after you release the lever.

4. If the caliper arms are too loose, they will vibrate excessively when you press the brake pads against the rim of the moving wheel. They should be as tight as they can be and still operate freely.

The tightness of lesser-quality calipers is controlled by a nut or pair of nuts on the front end of the mounting bolt. Because this part of the bolt functions as the pivot for the calipers, it is often referred to as the *pivot bolt*. If there are two nuts, the outer nut must be loosened and the pressure on the calipers must be adjusted with the inner one. Stop

Step 4

Step 5

tightening the inner nut just before the calipers start to show resistance to pivoting, then lock the two nuts against one another to maintain the adjustment (see photo on page 67).

5. If your brake has only a single nut or bolt head in front, turn that to adjust the caliper tension. Rotate the brake by hand to center the pads. Then hold the brake in that position while you tighten the mounting nut (see photo).

Squeeze the brake lever a few times to see if the brake pads are striking the rim at the same time and whether the brake remains centered after being used. If the brake needs minor centering and it's a modern dual-pivot model, look for a centering screw on top of or on each side of the caliper. Turning these small screws will move the brake slightly, centering it over the wheel.

6. On older sidepulls, hold the brake steady again while you snug up the mounting nut a bit more. Then turn both wrenches together to rock the entire brake body in the direction needed to center it.

Cantilever Installation and Adjustment

1. The cantilever brakes used on cyclocross bikes, some older mountain bikes, tandem bikes, and touring bikes are mounted differently than sidepull and conven-

Step 1

tional centerpull brakes. Each front cantilever is fastened by a bolt to a metal post brazed to the front of one of the fork legs (see photo). Cantilevers on the rear attach to posts brazed on the backs of the seatstays.

The brake pads on cantilevers are slightly different from those on caliper brakes. The posts that extend from the backs of the shoes on cantilevers are fairly long and are used to adjust the distance of the shoes from the rim.

2. When installing new cantilevers or readjusting an old set, make sure that the wheel is true and centered in the frame. Set all the brake pads equidistant from the rim. You'll probably need a hex key for the head of the pad mounting bolt and a combination wrench for the nut at its end (see photo).

Step 2

There are two factors to take into account in determining the proper setting of the pad. First, the pad should be turned so that it is parallel with the rim. Second, it should be set so it solidly contacts the rim when the arm is pushed toward the wheel. Too high and it may strike the tire; too low and it may dive into the spokes.

3. Cantilever brakes make use of a short cable—known as the linking, transverse, stirrup, or straddle cable—to connect the two braking arms. This cable may have a permanent fitting on only one end. If so, the other end is anchored by a bolt, and the cable length is adjustable.

Hook the end with the fitting into the cantilever arm that has a slot to receive it. Thread the other end through the anchor bolt found on the other arm. Where you anchor it depends in part on the frame. As a general rule, set the stirrup cable length such that when you pull up on its center, the angle is less than 90 degrees.

4. Give the main cable a light coating of grease, then push it through the housing, and seat the fitting on its upper end into the groove provided for it on the lever. Hook the center of the stirrup cable over the yoke and run the loose end of the main cable through its anchor bolt. If it's a Shimano cantilever, the cable may not end at the yoke—it may pass through it and end at the anchor on one brake arm.

Before anchoring the main cable at the yoke or the arm, thread the adjusting barrel at the lever end down almost against the lever to provide plenty of adjustment space as the cable stretches.

Step 5

5. Hold the cantilever arms against the wheel rim, pull the main cable taut, and tighten the bolt to anchor it (see photo). If the cable passed through the yoke on its way to the anchor on the brake arm, tighten the nut at the yoke, too, after making sure that both sides of the cable are the same length.

Squeeze the brake a few times. Adjust pad position and cable position if needed. If the brakes do not contact the rim at the same time, shift the position of the yoke along the stirrup cable toward the slower side. If that doesn't solve the problem, look for centering screws in the sides of the arms. Or release the stirrup wire to open the brake and rock the sticky arm away from the rim to increase the spring tension. Hook it back up.

Brake Help

Brake Pad Maintenance

Step 1

1. Keep brake pads close to and lined up with the rim so that when you brake, they don't hit the tire (causing a flat) or dive into the spokes (which might cause a crash). Bad pad alignment also causes poor braking as well as squeaking and chattering when braking. As the pads wear, they'll stop working properly, so it's important to maintain, inspect, and replace them regularly.

Different types of brakes use different pad designs, but they all need the same basic care. You need to keep them tight, aligned, and clean. Gravel travels up the rims, and small bits get pressed into the pads during braking. When enough grit gets in there, the pads become abrasive to the point that you can wear out your rims. Inspect the pads frequently, and use an awl or sharp tool to pick out any debris stuck in them (see photo). Remove the wheels first to make this easier.

2. Watch for uneven wear. Sometimes a pad will develop a lip if it's aligned too low or too high. This may cause the brake to stick. Refurbish the pad by trimming it flat with a utility knife (see photo). If it's a small defect, smooth it away with sandpaper.

Pad wear varies greatly. It's actually possible to wear out a set in a single off-road ride if it's muddy enough! They may last several years on a minimally used road bike, however.

Step 2

3. Most pads have grooves on them to help gauge wear (see photo). When the grooves begin to disappear, replace the pads. Also replace the pads anytime they are worn to the point that the metal pad holders are close to touching the rim. If the holders strike the rims, they'll damage the braking surface.

Step 3

4. There are two basic pad types: one-piece pads that must be unscrewed, and cartridge pads with rubber that can be pulled or pried out of a holder so you can slide in new ones.

The second type makes pad replacement faster and simpler, because popping in new ones doesn't require realigning the holders (meaning resetting the alignment to the rim). If your bike came with nonreplaceable pads, upgrade to replaceable pads once the old ones wear out.

To install a new one-piece pad, do one side at a time so you can compare the alignment and arrangement of the fastening pieces with the other side. Release the

Step 5

Step 6

Step 7

spring if you can, which will make alignment easier. Align the new pad so it strikes the rim squarely. On all brakes except direct-pull cantilevers, toe-in the pads very slightly. This means angling the pads so the front ends strike the rim first, which prevents squeaking.

5. Tighten each pad securely when it's set up right, then move on to the next. If you have a brake that the pads cannot be angled on by adjustment (usually basic sidepulls or center-pulls), upgrade to adjustable pads or achieve toe-in by gently bending the brake arms with an adjustable wrench. Sometimes, to get enough leverage, you need to use two adjustable wrenches, one on each arm. Use one to hold the brake steady while you bend with the other.

6. To install a cartridge-style pad, look for a set screw or small press-in pin holding the pad in place. If there isn't one, pry the old pad out by pressing a thin-blade screwdriver behind it and working the pad free. Then slide in a new pad. If it goes in tightly, press it in carefully with water-pump pliers.

7. If the pad has a retaining screw or pin, remove it, extract the pad, slide the new one in, and reinsert the pin. You may have to press on the end of the pad to get the pin to seat fully. When seated, the tip of the pin should be visible on the bottom of the pad holder.

WATCH THIS FIX:

FIND A STEP-BY-STEP VIDEO OF HOW TO INSTALL ROAD BRAKE PADS AT
www.bicycling.com/video/replace-and-adjust-brake-pad

Troubleshooting Rim Brakes

14 COMMON PROBLEMS, SOLVED!

PROBLEM: A pad drags on the rim or stays closer than the other pad.
SOLUTION: Check that the wheel is properly centered in the frame. Check that the wheel is true. Does the brake still stick? Center the brake. Still sticking? Check the pads. If one is worn unevenly, it may be catching on the rim. If so, carve or sand the pad flat.

PROBLEM: The brake squeaks.
SOLUTION: Make sure the pads are aligned correctly, and angle them so that the front tips touch the rims before the backs (this is called *toeing in* the pads). Still squeak? Try sanding the rims with medium emery cloth to remove buildup and roughen the surface.

PROBLEM: The brake feels mushy, and the levers must be squeezed too far.
SOLUTION: Check the pads for wear, and replace them if necessary. Make sure that the cable anchor bolt is tight. The cable may have stretched. Tighten the adjustment by turning the brake adjustment barrel on the lever or caliper counterclockwise.

PROBLEM: The brake is binding. You squeeze the lever, but the brake doesn't feel right. It's harder to pull the lever, and the brake doesn't snap back after you use it.
SOLUTION: Inspect the cables (also look inside the levers at the head of the cable) and housing sections (look for cracking and rust), and replace them if they're worn. If the cables are okay, try lubricating them with oil or grease. Also lubricate the pivot points on the brake.

PROBLEM: The bike brakes poorly.
SOLUTION: Check for oil on the rims and pads. Inspect the pads for wear, and replace them if necessary. Replace pads that are old, as they can harden with age and stop gripping the rim. Make sure the cables are in excellent shape; replace them if needed.

PROBLEM: You brake and get a grabby, jerky feel from the bike as it slows down.
SOLUTION: You may have a ding or dent in your rim. This will hit the brake on each revolution of the wheel, causing an unnerving jerky sensation. Remove the dent and get the rim as straight as possible. Replace the rim if it can't be fixed.

PROBLEM: The brake feels too tight. Squeezing and releasing the lever barely moves the brake.
SOLUTION: The cable adjustment is too tight. Look for a housing section that's twisted somehow or a housing end that's not seated in its frame stop. Housing okay? Try loosening the adjustment barrel at the lever or caliper (turn clockwise). Make sure there's at least a $\frac{1}{8}$-inch clearance between the pads and rims (you might need a little more than that on cantilever and direct-pull brakes).

PROBLEM: You installed cantilevers, and now one is tight on its post and won't pivot freely.
SOLUTION: You may have overtightened the bolt, which is bulging at the frame post it's screwed into, causing binding. Remove the bolt and brake arm, and sand the post until the brake fits on easily again. Don't overtighten the bolt.

PROBLEM: You've removed the cable for maintenance and discovered that the brake action is jammed. It seems stiff and barely moves when you try to squeeze it by hand.
SOLUTION: Corrosion has seized the brake. Dismantle it and sand the corrosion from the brake and brake mount(s) with sandpaper. Then lubricate all moving parts (keep lube away from the pads) and reassemble.

PROBLEM: You crashed and bent the brake or lever.
SOLUTION: If you can still ride, pedal home. If the part is seriously bent, replace it. It will break when you try to straighten it or, worse, when you're riding. If it's a minor bend, you may be able to carefully straighten the part by hand or with a pair of pliers.

PROBLEM: One cantilever brake pad sticks to the rim.
SOLUTION: If there is a triangular cable carrier at the end of the main brake cable,

try pushing it sideways on the transverse cable. When the carrier is out of position, it can cause one pad to hug the rim.

PROBLEM: You crashed and broke the cantilever brake. Now one side isn't attached to the frame.
SOLUTION: Usually this can be repaired with a cantilever repair kit, which includes everything needed to repair the frame post and reattach the cantilever. Ask your local shop about these kits.

PROBLEM: On long descents, you hear a disconcerting grating sound when braking steadily. It sounds like metal on metal, and the braking action is poor.
SOLUTION: Check the pads. They may have worn out, or you might have bad pads (even some new pads are inferior); replace them. The pads may have gotten contaminated by aluminum from the rim or have road grit embedded in their surfaces. Pick out the debris with an awl, or replace the pads.

PROBLEM: Turning the handlebar sideways causes the rear brake to grab the rim.
SOLUTION: The cable housing may be too short, or it may have gotten twisted somehow. Fix the housing so that you can turn the handlebar as needed without causing the brake to be applied.

CHAPTER 10

FRONT DERAILLEUR

How to adjust and maintain this simple chain mover

A well-maintained, properly installed front derailleur will shift the chain smoothly, accurately, and quickly. Here's what you need to know to make it happen.

WHAT'S IN THIS SECTION

- FRONT DERAILLEUR BASICS
- FRONT DERAILLEUR MAINTENANCE
- INSTALL A FRONT DERAILLEUR
- GET THE RIGHT DERAILLEUR!
- ADJUST A FRONT DERAILLEUR
- TROUBLESHOOTING FRONT DERAILLEURS

Front Derailleur Basics

Anatomy of a Front Derailleur

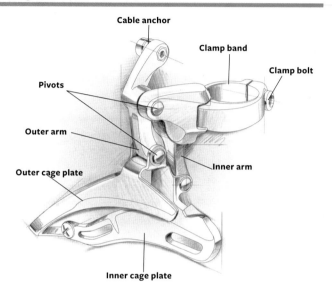

Cable anchor

Clamp band

Clamp bolt

Pivots

Outer arm

Inner arm

Outer cage plate

Inner cage plate

Cable Housing

Spiral-wound cable housing (below, top) is strong and flexible, but it compresses slightly as the cable inside is pulled taut. The precision involved in modern drivetrains makes linear or compressionless cable housing (below, bottom) necessary for accurate gear changes.

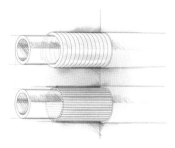

Front Derailleur Maintenance

1. A sluggish or difficult front derailleur requires a thorough cleaning. (If you're only lubing the derailleur's pivots, leave the derailleur on the bike so you can shift it back and forth while lubricant is applied.) To thoroughly clean a front derailleur, remove it from the bike and soak it in solvent. To do that, shift to take tension off the gear cable, then loosen the cable anchor bolt and disconnect the cable from the derailleur.

Step 2

2. Now get the chain out of the way. The simplest solution is to remove the pin that serves as a spacer between the tail ends of the two derailleur cage plates. Unscrew the bolt that holds the pin in place, remove the pin, and slip the chain out of the cage. No pin? Don't break the chain. Just slide the derailleur down the chain to where you can clean it easily.

Step 3

3. Remove the derailleur from the bike. Loosen and remove the bolt that fastens the derailleur's clamp to the seat tube or the derailleur to a braze-on mount. Put the bolt back into place in the derailleur (after the derailleur is removed) so you won't lose it.

4. Soak the derailleur in solvent to loosen the grit in its bearing areas. Give the lower part of the seat tube a cleaning, especially the area normally covered by the derailleur mounting clamp.

Use an old toothbrush or stiff brush to loosen any dirt that is clinging to the derailleur. Rinse the derailleur in the solvent once more, then wipe it clean with a rag. Let the clean derailleur sit for a while so the solvent evaporates.

Reattach the front derailleur exactly where it was before. Then reattach the gear cable to it. Squirt a little light oil or an appropriate spray lubricant into each of the derailleur's pivot points. Shift the derailleur and apply more lubricant. Shift the derailleur back and forth a few times to spread the lubricant around, then use a clean rag to wipe away any excess. Oil that is left on outer surfaces will attract fresh contaminants. Now, turn to page 81 for how to adjust the derailleur.

Install a Front Derailleur

1. Don't break the chain unless absolutely necessary. (Some front derailleurs have cages that can't be opened, in which case you do need to break the chain.) Simply remove the spacer from the tail of the derailleur cage, drop the cage down around the chain, and replace the spacer. However, if the chain is already broken, there is no need to remove the spacer pin. Just install the derailleur, run one end of the chain through it, and rejoin the ends of the chain. If the derailleur is equipped with a clamp, take out the clamp bolt and spread the jaws of the clamp band. Fit the clamp band around the seat tube of the bike at approximately the correct height, and replace the bolt.

Tighten the clamp bolt to prevent slipping but not so tight that it cannot be moved by hand.

2. If the derailleur is a braze-on model, fasten it securely to the braze-on mount, then partially loosen the height-adjusting bolt.

Before reattaching the gear cable, set the derailleur to the right height and angle. Keep the chain out of the way during these adjustments by slipping it off the chainring to the inside and letting it rest on the bottom bracket shell.

Step 2

Step 3

Pull the derailleur cage out over the large chainring, watching the outer plate of the cage as it passes over the chainring teeth. Adjust the derailleur height so that the cage clears the tallest chainring teeth by 1 to 3 millimeters.

3. Let go of the derailleur cage and sight down from above. Make sure the cage's outer plate is parallel to the chainring (see photo). Once both the height and horizontal alignment are set, tighten the clamp bolt.

4. Push the chain inside the derailleur cage, and wrap it around the small chainring. Fit the spacer back into the tail, and bolt it into place or rejoin the chain. Flush each section of derailleur housing with WD-40 or White Lightning Clean Streak (or install new housing), then thread a new gear cable through the shift lever and cable housing and route it to the front derailleur.

5. Run the cable through the anchor bolt on the derailleur and pull it taut. Hold the end of the cable with a pair of pliers while you tighten the anchor bolt. Push the shift lever a few times to stretch the cable, then loosen the bolt, take up any slack, and retighten.

Get the Right Derailleur!

Some bikes are set up so the cable runs above the bottom bracket on the way to the front derailleur, others run the cable below the bottom bracket, and still others route the cable from the top down. Also, note that some front derailleurs are designed to receive open cable; others have a cable-housing stop and are designed to be used with a section of housed cable. If your new derailleur is not compatible with your bike, return to the shop and get the correct one.

6. Cut the new cable with a sharp pair of cable cutters, leaving approximately 1 to $1\frac{1}{2}$ inches of wire extending beyond the anchor bolt. Crimp a cap on the cable end to prevent fraying.

After installing a front derailleur, follow the steps below to make sure that it is properly adjusted before riding the bicycle.

WATCH THIS FIX:

FIND A STEP-BY-STEP VIDEO OF HOW TO INSTALL A FRONT DERAILLEUR AT www.bicycling.com/video/install-front-derailleur

Adjust a Front Derailleur

1. The first step in adjusting a new or mis-shifting front derailleur is to set its range of motion.

Begin by shifting the chain to the inside onto the small chainring and largest cassette cog. Locate the adjusting screw for setting the inner stop on the derailleur. Derailleurs with limit screws arranged horizontally come in two basic types: traditional and top swing. If the derailleur is a braze-on type or the frame clamp is above the cage, this is a traditional derailleur, and the inner limit screw is the one closest to the frame. If the frame clamp is below the top of the cage, this is a top-swing derailleur, and the screws are reversed. Fortunately, top-swing derailleurs usually have the screws labeled "high" and "low" to reduce confusion. If they are positioned vertically, it will probably be the one on top. Turn the screw in or out as needed, until the inner plate of the derailleur cage is held 2 millimeters from the inside of the chain.

2. Shift the chain to the outside, onto the large chainring and the smallest rear cog. Set the other adjusting screw so the outer plate of the cage is held about 2 millimeters outside the chain.

These settings should allow you to shift between chainrings with no rubbing of

Step 2

Step 3

Step 4

the chain and derailleur cage after the shift. Test the adjustments with the bike still on the repair stand. If the chain rubs at all on the inside with the first setting or on the outside with the second, these limits have to be expanded. But don't set them so wide that the chain comes off the chainring during a rapid shift (check for this!), and in no case should the derailleur move so far out that it strikes the crankarm.

3. If your front derailleur gives sloppy shifting, look closely at its shape. Most manufacturers bend the front ends of the cage plates slightly in toward one another to create a narrow nose for more authoritative shifting. If your derailleur needs its nose narrowed, use a pair of pliers to gently toe-in the plates.

4. Sometimes, when a shift is made with the rear derailleur, the change of chain angle causes the chain to rub the tail end of one of the front derailleur cage plates (see photo). This is especially common on a bike with a narrow derailleur cage and 9, 10, or 11 cogs. The rubbing will eventually wear out the derailleur. Usually, all it takes to remedy the problem is slightly moving the left (or front) shift lever, which is called *trimming* the derailleur.

5. If you want to eliminate or reduce chain rub after rear shifts, you can widen the back of your derailleur cage a bit. (This is not possible if you have a derailleur with a cage that cannot be opened.) Partially remove the bolt holding the spacer pin in the tail of the cage. Slip a small washer between the spacer and the inner plate of the cage, and retighten the bolt.

One final problem: chain drag on the tail pin in certain gear combinations. For example, shifting the chain onto both a small chainring and a small rear cog drops it low in the cage, which may cause it to drag. The solution is simple: Don't use the chain in this gear combination.

Chain drag may also result from a mismatch between the front derailleur and the chainrings, such as using a tiny inner chainring with a derailleur designed for a sport touring bike. The solution here should be obvious: If you intend to use extra-small chainrings, equip your bike with a derailleur that is designed for them. No mechanical adjustment can compensate for mismatched chainrings and derailleurs.

WATCH THIS FIX:

FIND A STEP-BY-STEP VIDEO OF ADJUSTING A FRONT DERAILLEUR AT
www.bicycling.com/video/adjust-front-derailleur

Troubleshooting Front Derailleurs

8 COMMON PROBLEMS, SOLVED!

PROBLEM: While you're riding, the chain falls off when you shift to the small chainring.
SOLUTION: Pedal very gently and shift the derailleur back to the large chainring. With luck, the chain will shift onto the chainring. If the problem is chronic, check the adjustment of the inner limit screw.

PROBLEM: When you stand to climb, the chain rubs the derailleur.
SOLUTION: Adjust the low-gear adjusting screw so there's more clearance between the cage and the chain.

PROBLEM: When you stand to sprint, the chain rubs the derailleur.
SOLUTION: The chainring may be slightly bent. Sight it and have it trued if it's bent. Or adjust the high-gear adjusting screw to give more clearance between the cage and the chain when in high gear.

PROBLEM: The derailleur won't shift to the smaller chainring.
SOLUTION: Make sure the cable is moving smoothly. Check that the angle of the cage is parallel to the chainrings, that the low-gear adjusting screw allows the derailleur to move far enough to the inside, and that the nose of the derailleur is slightly bent toward the chain.

PROBLEM: The derailleur won't shift to the large chainring.
SOLUTION: Check that the angle of the cage is parallel to the chainrings, the high-gear adjusting screw allows the derailleur to move far enough to the outside, and the cage's nose is slightly bent toward the chain.

PROBLEM: The derailleur won't shift to the middle ring on a triple chainring.
SOLUTION: Make sure that the chainring is correctly installed. If it's upside down or the spacers are incorrect, the chain won't be able to find the chainring.

PROBLEM: The anchor bolt got stripped when you tightened it.
SOLUTION: Try tapping it to a larger bolt diameter and installing a larger bolt.

PROBLEM: The chain rubbed a hole in the cage.
SOLUTION: If possible, install a new cage. Or replace the derailleur. Don't allow the chain to rub and wear out the new derailleur.

CHAPTER 10

CRANKSET AND BOTTOM BRACKET

Removal, maintenance, and replacement of the most common setups

Cranksets and bottom brackets (BBs) on most performance bikes generally fall into two categories: a two-piece design, where the BB spindle is integrated into one arm of the crankset, and the more traditional spindle-BB design, where the crankarms are attached to a spindle (usually square taper or splined) integrated into the BB.

Here, we'll show you how to identify, maintain, and overhaul a variety of both types of designs. Enjoy!

WHAT'S IN THIS SECTION

- CRANKSET AND BOTTOM BRACKET BASICS
- REMOVE AND INSTALL A SHIMANO TWO-PIECE CRANKSET
- REMOVE AND INSTALL SRAM AND TRUVATIV GXP CRANKSETS
- REMOVE AND INSTALL AN FSA EXTERNAL CRANKSET
- REMOVE AND INSTALL CAMPAGNOLO OVER TORQUE CRANKSETS
- REMOVE AND INSTALL CAMPAGNOLO AND FULCRUM ULTRA-TORQUE CRANKSETS
- INSTALL A SEALED-BEARING CARTRIDGE-STYLE BOTTOM BRACKET
- CHAINRING MAINTENANCE
- CRANKSET MAINTENANCE
- TROUBLESHOOTING CRANKSETS AND BOTTOM BRACKETS

Crankset and Bottom Bracket Basics

Anatomy of a Crank and Bottom Bracket

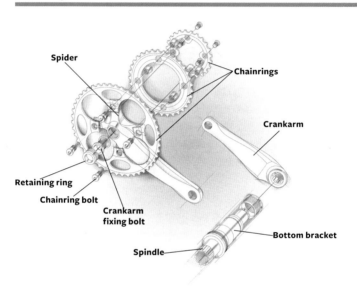

Spider

Chainrings

Crankarm

Retaining ring

Chainring bolt

Crankarm fixing bolt

Bottom bracket

Spindle

Identifying Two-Piece, Splined, and Square Taper Designs

External or two-piece: A modern standard used with two-piece cranksets; the bearing cups sit outside the BB shell, and the spindle is part of the cranks. This is the most common design on new bikes.

Square taper: An older-style crank interface; easy to spot with the four-sided crank interface.

Shimano Octalink: A Shimano standard for splined crank interfaces.

ISIS: A splined standard agreed upon by a number of manufacturers, including Race Face (shown here).

Remove and Install a Shimano Two-Piece Crankset

1. Loosen the two pinch bolts on the left crankarm with a 5-millimeter hex key. These bolts clamp the arm in place on the spindle.

2. Use Shimano's crankarm installation tool (TL-FC16), or Park Tool's version of it (the BBT-9), to remove the preload cap by turning it counterclockwise. The left crankarm will slip easily off the spindle.

Step 2

3. Notice that there is a broad spline on the spindle and inside the crankarm, making it nearly impossible to misalign the left crankarm when you reinstall it. There is also a thin black rubber O-ring on the spindle between the bearing and crankarm. Remove this from the spindle and set it into its seat on the crankarm to keep track of it.

Step 3

Step 5

4. The spindle will now smoothly slide out of the bottom bracket. If it's not cooperating, give the end of the spindle a few light taps with a rubber mallet.

5. Remove the bottom bracket cups from the shell using an appropriate spanner. Shimano's part number for this tool is TL-FC32; Park Tool's BBT-9 will also work. Most road and mountain bikes today have an English-thread BB shell, so the left-side cup will come out when turned counterclockwise, but the right-side cup must be turned clockwise to remove it.

Installation is as simple as reversing these steps. Don't overtighten the preload cap that holds the left crankarm in place. This cap is intended only to snug the crankarm in place and should be only slightly more than finger-tight. Finally, tighten the pinch bolts incrementally to be sure they are both properly and evenly torqued.

Remove and Install SRAM and Truvativ GXP Cranksets

Step 1

1. To remove the left arm, loosen the crank-fixing bolt with an 8-millimeter hex key until you feel resistance again. At this point, the bolt is pushing outward. Continue turning the bolt counterclockwise until the arm frees itself from the spline on the spindle.

2. With the left arm removed, you can slide the spindle out of the bottom bracket by pulling on the right crankarm. If it's tight, gently tap it with a plastic mallet to free it.

3. Notice that there is a change in diameter on the end of the spindle. This shoulder traps the left-side bearing against the left crankarm. This simple feature puts the task of stabilizing the crankset onto the left-side bearing, so the right-side bearing can float freely on the spindle with no side load. The floating design eliminates unnecessary drag in the system.

Step 2

4. The cups are removed and installed in the same manner as any other external bottom bracket. Using a wrench for external-type BB cups, turn the left side counterclockwise to remove it. Turn the right-side cup clockwise to remove it.

The exception: Some Italian frames have Italian-threaded BB shells. If the bearing cup is marked with the word *Italian,* turns it counterclockwise, regardless of which side of the frame it occupies.

Step 4

5. Installation is simple. Clean the threads in the BB shell, lightly grease the threads on the cups, and determine whether spacers are necessary (for mountain bike cranksets) before threading the cups into the shell. If you have an Italian-threaded frame, be sure you check the cups and install the one marked "nondrive" on the left side of the frame. Otherwise, the spindle won't fit correctly.

Position the chain so it won't get trapped, then slip the spindle through the BB until it stops. Align the left crankarm on the spline and tighten the fixing bolt until the arm bottoms out on the left-side bearing. That's it. Really.

Remove and Install an FSA External Crankset

1. FSA cranksets come in two varieties: Some models have pinch bolts to affix the left arm to the spindle, and some don't.

    If your crankset is a Gossamer model, it has pinch bolts on the left arm. Loosen the pinch bolts and then remove the preload cap from the face of the arm. With the preload cap removed, the arm should slide easily from the spindle.

Step 2

2. SL-K model cranksets don't have pinch bolts and instead rely on a precision-fit spline. The fixing bolt also functions as the extractor. Turn the bolt counterclockwise to loosen it. You'll feel resistance again, but keep turning until the arm frees itself from the spindle.

Step 3

3. SL-K cranks have a wave washer on the spindle, between the left arm and the bottom bracket. Insignificant as it may look, this is a critical part for maintaining the proper bearing preload.

    Gossamer cranks sometimes also have a special washer. In this case, the washer is specific to the model of BB rather than to the crankset. You can find out which BB models require washers by consulting your local shop or checking out the tech documents on FSA's Web site (www.fullspeedahead.com).

4. With the left arm removed, the spindle will slide out of the BB with a tug on the spider. If it's snug, a few gentle taps with a plastic mallet will set it free.

    Remove the cups from the BB shell by turning the left cup counterclockwise and the right cup clockwise (unless it's Italian-threaded).

5. Installation begins by putting the cups back in. Make sure the threads in the bottom bracket shell are clean and free of burrs, lightly grease the threads on the cups, and determine whether spacers are necessary before threading the cups into the shell.

If your Gossamer-type crank and bottom bracket combination requires crush washers, make sure one is installed on the spindle. Push the spindle through the BB until the right arm butts against the right-side bearing. SLK-type cranks do not require a washer on the right side.

6. Before installing the left arm, put the wave washer (SLK) or crush washer (if necessary for your Gossamer crank–BB) on the exposed end of the spindle.

7. For SLK models, align the left arm on the end of the spindle and tighten it in place with the fixing bolt. At this point, SL-K cranks are fully installed.

Step 6

A Gossamer left crankarm will slip onto the spindle by hand. Once it's in place, install and snug the preload cap.

8. Finish the Gossamer crankset installation by tightening the pinch bolts. Tighten in small increments—one, then the other, and back to the first. Repeat this until both bolts are properly torqued.

Remove and Install Campagnolo Over Torque Cranksets

1. Campagnolo Over Torque cranksets, introduced in late 2013, are similar to other two-piece cranksets in that a splined bottom-bracket spindle is attached to the drive-side crankarm, and adjustments are managed via the non-drive-side arm.

However, a few key differences set Over Torque apart, and we'll cover those differences here.

Step 2

2. To remove the crankarm, first unlock the dowel on the clearance recovery ring (a small black ring between the left crankarm and the bottom bracket shell) using a 1.5-millimeter Allen wrench, and turn the ring counterclockwise to loosen it slightly.

Step 3

3. Now, use the crankarm removal tool (UT-FC130) to remove the lock ring around the center of the left-hand crank. The pins in the tool align with the holes in the ring; use an 8-millimeter Allen wrench to turn the tool and remove the ring.

4. Use the other side of the tool to remove the crankarm itself. First, back out the inner drum so that you can easily slide the tool over the crankarm without scratching it. Slide the tool in place over the crankarm, then use an 8-millimeter Allen wrench to tighten the exterior bolt on the tool. Turning the tool in will force the crankarm off the bottom bracket spindle. Once it's off, loosen the bolt to remove the crankarm from the tool. Slide off the clearance recovery ring, and then pull the drive-side crankarm out from the bottom bracket, keeping track of any spacers used to match your bottom bracket width.

Step 4

5. Installation follows the same basic steps but in reverse and using the UT-FC220 installation tool. Put a light coating of grease on the gaskets of the bottom bracket cups, and put any necessary spacers in place (you kept track when you removed the BB, didn't you?).

6. Position the clearance recovery ring on the non-drive-side spindle, with the teeth of the ring facing out. Put a coating of grease on the end of the spindle and inside the crankarm, and put the crankarm in position on the spindle.

7. Put the installation tool (UT-FC220) in place (make sure the interior drum is protruding slightly) using a 5-millimeter Allen wrench. Then, using a 24-millimeter wrench or socket, tighten the tool until the end of the BB spindle is flush with the crankarm. Remove the tool with the Allen wrench.

8. Fit the lockring, and use the UT-FC130 tool to tighten it in place. Use a torque wrench and tighten the lockring to 8 to 10 NM of force. Tighten the clearance recovery ring (between the left crankarm and the BB shell) to take out any remaining play—it should be only finger-tight—then turn the dowel with a 1.5-millimeter Allen wrench to lock it into position. Done.

Step 7

Remove and Install Campagnolo and Fulcrum Ultra-Torque Cranksets

1. On Campagnolo and Fulcrum Ultra-Torque cranksets, the spindle is in two halves, each permanently affixed to a crankarm. A spline on the end of each spindle segment joins with the other in the center of the bottom bracket with a

Step 1

Step 2

Step 3

substantial bolt holding the assembly together. A 10-millimeter hex key on a 2-inch ratchet extender can reach inside the right side of the spindle to access the bolt.

2. Removing the bolt frees the left arm for removal. Notice that the bearing is press-fitted onto the spindle, rather than into the cup, as is the case with other two-piece designs.

There is also a wave washer that fits inside the cup to preload the bearing.

3. Remove the retaining clip from the right-side cup to remove the right arm and spindle segment. The clip is tricky to get at. Pull one side of the clip out with needle-nose pliers, then repeat on the other side. The right crankarm should slip out of the cup.

4. Remove the cups from the BB shell as you would any other external-type cups. Turn the left-side cup counterclockwise and the right-side cup clockwise (unless it's Italian-threaded).

Installation is a straightforward reversal of these steps. Make sure the threads in the BB shell are clean and free of burrs, and lightly grease the threads on the cups before threading the cups into the shell.

5. The Ultra-Torque spline should be liberally greased before pushing the right crankarm and spindle segment into the right-side BB cup.

6. Reinstall the retaining clip on the right-side BB cup. Insignificant as it may seem, the clip plays a crucial role by securely holding the right-side bearing in position in its cup, stabilizing the system so the crankset can't float side to side in the BB. Floating can cause front shifting problems or possibly throw the chain.

Step 7

7. Place the wave washer in the left-side BB cup and then slide the left crankarm and spindle segment into the cup. Be sure the splines align and engage properly, then prepare for a good arm workout.

8. Put the crank-fixing bolt on the end of the extender, insert it into the right-side spindle, and tighten it until you feel the assembly bottom out.

Step 8

Install a Sealed-Bearing Cartridge-Style Bottom Bracket

Note: There are many different sealed-bearing cartridge-style bottom bracket designs, with more coming along almost daily. If these instructions don't match your BB, visit the manufacturer's Web site for installation details.

1. Remove the old bottom bracket. It might be as easy as turning the cartridge out with the splined removal tool. Turn the left-side cup first, counterclockwise, until it comes out of the frame. Then turn the right-side cup clockwise to remove the cartridge.

If the cups won't turn, don't force them. Apply Liquid Wrench or a similar penetrating lubricant to the cup edges and tap the BB shell with a hammer to vibrate it, which should work the solvent into the threads. Wait a while and try to turn the cups again. Repeat this procedure until the cups unscrew, or take the bike to a shop for help.

Sealed cartridge BBs come from the factory packed with grease and adjusted. Before installing the new one, turn the spindle by hand to feel how the factory adjustment feels. Later, when it's installed, the spindle should turn much as it does fresh from the box.

Cartridge bottom brackets usually have one cup preinstalled on the drive side of the cartridge. If the BB is being installed in a titanium frame, coat the threads with Finish Line Ti-Prep or some other anti-seize compound. Wrapping plumber's Teflon tape around the threads of the cartridge and cup is also acceptable.

Step 2

2. Treating the threads will prevent chronic clicking noises from the bottom bracket area and fight galvanic corrosion, which can freeze the BB into the shell. (Grease is usually adequate for steel and aluminum frames.)

Start threading the cartridge into the drive side of the frame by hand-turning it counterclockwise (see photo). Be careful not to cross-thread it.

Step 3

3. When the cartridge gets tough to turn, install the splined tool (see photo) and continue turning until the cup is snug and fully screwed into the frame (it'll go only so far because of the built-in lip on the cup edge).

4. Install the other cup (be careful not to cross-thread it), turning it clockwise with the splined tool until the cup bottoms against the cartridge. Check how things are going by turning the spindle by hand. If it's a lot tighter than it was before installation, it's likely that the cup is going in crooked. Remove it and start again, making sure it's straight. When the cup is secure, check the installation by putting the splined tool on the drive side again and making sure it's tight, then double-check the tightness of the left-side cup. Finally, grab the spindle and turn it. It should feel smooth, like it did before installation. If not, try again.

When the bottom bracket is installed correctly, attach the crankarms. Remember to snug the bolts after the first ride and monthly thereafter.

Chainring Maintenance

1. Keep them clean. At least once a month—more often if you do a lot of riding on wet and dirty terrain—take a rag and wipe your chainrings clean. Dampen the rag with a little solvent, if you need to, or use a stiff brush to loosen the grime so it can be wiped away. Clean your chain at the same time, or this work will be for nothing. See page 104 for instructions.

2. Keep them straight. Straightening a bent chainring can be managed with a hammer or the help of a chainring bending tool. This is a simple tool, one that is less expensive than most specialized bike tools. To pry out a bent tooth or an extreme bend in a ring, you can also use an adjustable wrench after tightening the jaws enough that they just slip over the ring.

3. Check for wear. If you see shiny cuts on the sides of the chainring teeth, it means you're riding in gear combinations that force the chain into extreme angles. One extreme occurs when you ride with the chain on the large chainring and the largest inner cog. Another results from the chain being shifted onto the inner chainring and the smallest rear cog.

4. Replace as needed. Replacing worn chainrings is usually an easy process. Normally, they're attached with hex key bolts to a five-armed spider that radiates out from the base of the right crankarm. Simply remove the five bolts (if they're stuck, hold their backs with a flat-blade screwdriver) while holding the ring in place, then slide it off the crankarm. Slide on a new ring and bolt it in place (always grease the bolts first). Large or outer chainrings often have a pin extending from the side near one of the bolt holes. Take care to line up this pin with the crankarm, since the chainring features pickup ramps specially located to enhance shifting performance. Those ramps work best when properly aligned with the power portion of the pedal stroke.

5. Keep it tight. Periodically, check that your chainring bolts are tight. You might even want to carry the necessary wrench in a small tool kit when you travel on your bike.

Crankset Maintenance

1. Check the bolts. Check the tightness of the crankarm bolts at the end of the first ride after their installation and monthly after that. Check for loose pedals at the same time.

2. Check the BB. Tug on the cranks to see if the bottom bracket adjustment has loosened. Sealed cartridge BBs are okay with a bit of play. Lots of play, however, indicates that something is wrong—possibly that the BB is worn out.

3. Beware of bends! If the crankarms get bent (in an accident, for example), only steel ones can be safely bent back. Bent aluminum models should be replaced, because they usually break when straightened (sometimes well after being straightened). Bent spiders can be straightened in many cases, even on aluminum cranksets. This work is best left to a bike mechanic. Without the proper tools and knowledge, you might further damage the components.

4. Overcome stripping! If you misuse the crankarm removal tool, the result is usually stripped crankarm threads, which means it's impossible to remove the crankarm with the tool. However, you can remove it without the tool. Remove the bolt, and ride around the neighborhood for a while. Eventually, the crankarm will loosen and come right off. Another option: Your bike shop might have a Stein or

Var crank extractor system specifically designed to pull crankarms with stripped threads. Bear in mind that a crankarm with stripped extractor threads can be reinstalled on a bike, but it can never be rethreaded and will require special extractors to remove. Consider buying new.

5. Pedal problem? It's possible to strip the pedal threads in the crankarm. It usually happens when you force the wrong pedal into an aluminum crankarm. Sometimes it's possible to repair this problem, though it's a job for a shop with the right tools.

Troubleshooting Cranksets and Bottom Brackets

9 COMMON PROBLEMS, SOLVED!

PROBLEM: The large chainring flexes, causing the chain to always rub against the front derailleur cage.
SOLUTION: Check for loose chainring bolts. Get the chainring straightened if it's bent. If you find nothing wrong, then try pedaling faster (about 90 rpm is a good goal), which will put less pressure on the chainring and flex it less.

PROBLEM: There's a trace of play in your sealed bottom bracket.
SOLUTION: Tighten the retaining cup/ring; it may have loosened slightly in the frame.

PROBLEM: There's a creaking sound when you pedal.
SOLUTION: Tighten the crankarm bolts. If the arm still creaks, remove it, apply a trace of grease to the spindle, and reinstall the arm.

PROBLEM: You removed the chainrings to clean the crankset and now the front derailleur doesn't shift right.
SOLUTION: You may have installed a chainring backward. Remove the rings and put them on correctly. Usually, the crankarm bolts fit into indentations on the chainrings. Sight from above, too, to make sure there's even spacing between the rings.

PROBLEM: You're trying to remove the chainring bolt, but it just spins.
SOLUTION: Hold the back half of the chainring bolt with a chainring bolt wrench or a wide flat-blade screwdriver.

PROBLEM: There's a knocking sound when you pedal.
SOLUTION: If you have a sealed cartridge BB, moisture may have penetrated the threads between the bottom bracket and the shell, causing light corrosion. This is most common with aluminum BB shells, but it's not unusual to experience it with steel or titanium. Remove the crank and BB, clean the threads of both with a wire brush, apply fresh grease or anti-seize compound (using anti-seize or Ti-Prep for titanium frames), or wrap plumber's Teflon tape over the threads and reinstall the BB. For those with a nonsealed bottom bracket, a knocking sound usually comes from a loose fixed cup (the right-side one). Tighten it securely by turning it counterclockwise.

PROBLEM: You stripped the crankarm threads, and now you can't remove the crankarm.
SOLUTION: Ride the bike around the block a few times. The crankarm will loosen, and you'll be able to take it off. Or take it to a shop, which may have special tools to remove cranks with stripped extractor threads.

PROBLEM: You crashed into a rock and bent the chainring.
SOLUTION: On the trail, try pounding it straight with a rock. At home, use an adjustable wrench (make the jaws just wide enough to grab the ring) to pry the ring back into place. If it's seriously bent, replace it.

PROBLEM: You broke a tooth off the chainring.
SOLUTION: Don't worry about it. It should still work okay. If it's causing the chain to run rough, file down any protruding pieces.

PART 4 / DRIVETRAIN

CHAPTER 11

CHAIN

The basics of cleaning, removing, and replacing a key drivetrain component

As drivetrains add gears (we're at 11 speeds and counting!), chains are becoming more highly engineered. They're now precision instruments that require more care—and that's where the following guidance will help.

WHAT'S IN THIS SECTION

- CHAIN BASICS
- CURE CHAINSUCK
- CLEAN A CHAIN
- REMOVE A QUICK-CONNECT CHAIN
- REMOVE A CHAIN
- INSTALL A CHAIN
- TROUBLESHOOTING CHAINS

Chain Basics

Anatomy of a Chain

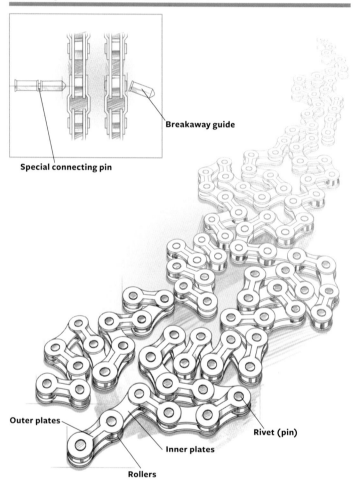

Special connecting pin

Breakaway guide

Outer plates

Inner plates

Rivet (pin)

Rollers

Measure for Wear

If you have a new 10- or 11-speed drivetrain and chain, invest in a chain checker. This inexpensive device can alert you to chain wear before it eats your drivetrain. A less-precise option: Measure out 24 pins on your chain, from the center of the first pin to the center of the last. It should measure 12 inches. When the measurement hits $1^{23}/_{32}$ inches, install a new chain. Beyond $12^{1}/_{8}$ inch? You might need new chainrings and cogs, too.

Cure Chainsuck

There are two common causes of chainsuck: a dirty drivetrain and bent chainring teeth. If chainsuck happens to you, clean your chainrings thoroughly, and while you're at it, inspect them for damaged teeth. Bend them back into position if necessary. Thoroughly lube (and wipe down) the drivetrain before riding again.

Be Quick with Connectors

SRAM, KMC, and Wippermann manufacture chains with master links that slide apart, making a chain tool unnecessary (but carry a spare link in case your chain breaks on a ride). KMC also offers their master link, called the MissingLink, as an aftermarket product that comes in versions for most chains. SRAM also offers replacement PowerLink and PowerLock connectors, though they specifically recommend that these be used only on SRAM-brand chains. These special links are easy to spot, because they look different than the other links on the chain. Note that to handle the additional stresses on narrower, more flexible 10-speed chains, SRAM has developed the PowerLock link that snaps together and isn't meant to be disassembled.

Clean a Chain

1. Cleaning and lubricating can usually be performed without disassembling the chain.

Wipe the chain down about once a week, or after any especially wet or muddy ride, with a rag soaked with a small amount of solvent. Allow the chain to air-dry before applying fresh lubricant. Drip lubricant onto the bushings and gaps where the inner and outer side plates meet.

Turn the crank backward a few revolutions to work the lubricant into the chain so it can coat the pins—where most wear occurs.

Finally, wipe excess lubricant from the outside of the chain with a dry rag. The outside of the chain needs only a thin film of lubricant to protect it from corrosion.

Step 2

2. If your chain is really grimy, clean it with a special combination brush-and-reservoir system (such as Park Tool's CM-5 Cyclone Chain Scrubber) while on the bike.

WATCH THIS FIX:

FIND A STEP-BY-STEP VIDEO OF HOW TO CLEAN AND LUBE A CHAIN AT
www.bicycling.com/video/clean-and-lubricate-chain

Remove a Quick-Connect Chain

1. Quick-connect chains like SRAM's PowerLink Connector models make it simple and convenient to remove your chain for cleaning without the use of tools.

To begin, find the special connecting link. Some manufacturers make this link a different color so it's easy to find. In all cases, the connecting link can be identified by elongated holes in the side plates.

Note: If the connecting link is colored black on your 10-speed chain, this may be a SRAM PowerLock link, which isn't meant to be disassembled.

Pinch the side plates toward each other with your fingers. This frees the ends of the pins from recesses in the side plates.

Step 2

2. With the side plates pinched together, slide the pins toward each other. Each pin will move through the elongated hole in the opposite side plate to the release position.

3. Separate the connecting link by moving the side plates away from one another. Reconnect the chain by reversing these steps.

Step 3

Remove a Chain

1. You'll need a special chain tool (sometimes called a *chain breaker*) to separate a link.

Slip the chain off the chainring to remove tension. Wind the center rod of the chain tool back far enough for a link of chain to slip into the slot provided for it, then screw the rod forward against the pin (see photo).

Step 1

Make sure that the rod and pin are properly aligned. Continue to wind the rod forward to push out the pin.

Step 2

2. Some older chains can be disassembled and reassembled using the same pin. To do this, don't push the pin all the way out, as it's nearly impossible to reinsert. Watch the pin closely, and when you think it's most of the way through, unwind the chain tool and flex the chain sideways to separate it. If it won't come apart the first time, carefully repeat the steps, incrementally, until it does.

3. Shimano chains require that you push the pin out entirely and replace it with a special, hardened replacement pin. Campagnolo goes one step further and makes a kit of several links that replace a short segment of the chain to ensure an ideal connection. Find the pin where the chain was initially connected. It will usually have a different finish than the rest or sometimes a dimple. Break the chain as near to opposite this pin as you can estimate. Shimano and Campagnolo both recommend that a chain should not be broken and reassembled more than once after installation, so do this only if you think it's absolutely necessary.

Install a Chain

1. A general rule when installing a new chain is that it should be long enough to permit shifting onto the largest cassette cog while also on the largest chainring. This will prevent damage to the derailleurs in the event that you unintentionally shift into this normally unused combination. The rear derailleur should be almost fully extended at this point. Once you have the right length, use a chain tool (and the steps outlined on page 105, in Remove a Chain) to get the chain down to size.

Be aware that some newer Shimano chains (CN-7900 and CN-6700, for example) are asymmetrical and should be installed on the bike with the engraved *Shimano* plates facing out. Shimano additionally recommends a specific direction for the chain. Holding the chain in front of you, the inner-plate end should be in your left hand and the outer-plate end in your right hand before installing it on the bike.

Step 1

2. Align the ends, and use the chain tool to force the pin in. If it's a Shimano or Campagnolo special pin, it should be installed from the inboard side of the bike to the outside for the strongest connection; it will make a slight clicking sound when it's seated. After that, you'll need to remove the guide end of the pin (break it off with pliers if it is a one-piece pin and guide). Only Campagnolo 11-speed chains require the additional step of flaring the ends of the replacement pins using their special UN-CT300 chain tool.

If the rejoined link is stiff, flex it back and forth sideways to loosen it. Mount the chain on the chainring, and lubricate.

Troubleshooting Chains

8 COMMON PROBLEMS, SOLVED!

PROBLEM: The chain is always a black, grimy mess.
SOLUTION: Clean it, and use less lube or a lighter onr.

PROBLEM: The chain squeaks when you pedal, even though you've lubed it.
SOLUTION: Try a lube with better penetrating qualities. After applying it, let it sit for a while. Wipe off excess lube, because it will attract dirt.

PROBLEM: When you pedal hard, the chain skips.
SOLUTION: The chain may be worn out. Measure the chain with a chain wear indicator and replace it if necessary. If the chain isn't worn, it may be a tight link. Find it by pedaling backward and watching for it to bind as it passes through the derailleur pulleys. Then flex the chain sideways to free the link. If the chain checks out okay and the problem still persists, inspect your cogs and chainrings for bent or broken teeth, and replace as necessary.

PROBLEM: The chain runs rough when you pedal.
SOLUTION: Replace it if it's worn out, or try a different model of chain if yours is relatively new but runs rough. Some chains run smoother than others. It may also be a worn cog or chainring (if the teeth are smallish and hook-shaped, they're worn).

PROBLEM: A few chain links got bent.
SOLUTION: Try straightening them by twisting the chain with pliers. Or replace them with new links (be sure to use the same type).

PROBLEM: The chain runs noisily.
SOLUTION: If the chain is lubed and not worn, it's probably a derailleur adjustment problem.

PROBLEM: The chain falls off all the time.
SOLUTION: This is usually a derailleur adjustment problem. See page 90.

PROBLEM: When you shift, the chain gets jammed between the chainrings.
SOLUTION: Make sure that the chain is the right width for the drivetrain. If it is, check the chainring bolts for tightness. Make sure the chainrings are straight. Check their spacing, and replace any worn ones.

CHAPTER 12

CASSETTE

Care and maintenance of cogs that deliver power to the rear wheel

In this section, we cover how to select and care for the cassette—the collection of cogs on the rear hub. What we don't cover: freewheels, the old-fashioned setup that uses thread-on cogs. Most bikes built since about 1980 use cassettes. They're easier to remove and install, and they allow for stiffer, stronger hub construction. Win!

WHAT'S IN THIS SECTION

- CASSETTE BASICS
- CASSETTE MAINTENANCE
- COMPATIBILITY
- CASSETTE REMOVAL AND DISASSEMBLY
- TROUBLESHOOTING CASSETTES

Cassette Basics

Anatomy of a Cassette

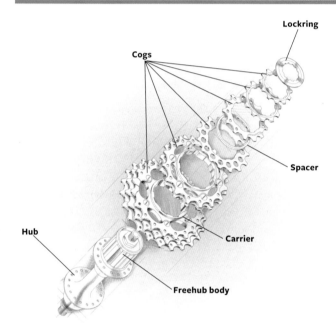

Lockring

Cogs

Spacer

Carrier

Hub

Freehub body

Cassette Maintenance

1. This is all about cleaning and lubrication. We recommend that this be done at least monthly. If you ride in a heavy rainstorm, clean and lubricate both your chain and cassette.

Want to do a thorough cleaning job? Remove the wheel, then lay it down on a workbench or other flat surface to free both your hands for cleaning.

Use a rag to wipe the grime off the surface of the cogs. Moisten the rag with solvent if necessary. After cleaning the outer surface of the first cog, hold the rag with both hands. Pull it taut and slide it between successive cogs, cleaning both sides of each with a shoeshine motion.

2. Make sure to also clean the troughs between teeth. If you have difficulty getting the cogs clean with a rag alone, use a stiff brush (like a toothbrush) to loosen the grime, and use the rag to wipe it away.

Clean the teeth of the cogs as well as you can. When the chain pulls against those teeth, any leftover grit

Step 2

Compatibility

Generally speaking, SRAM, Shimano, and other aftermarket 8-, 9-, and 10-speed cassettes can fit on the same freehub body. Campagnolo 9-, 10-, and 11-speed cassettes use their own freehub design. Shimano 11-speed cassettes also require wider freehub bodies. And SRAM's XX1—a mountain bike drivetrain with an 11-speed cassette and a single chainring—requires a specific freehub, as well. Bottom line? If you're changing drivetrains, talk to your local bike shop to make sure everything is compatible.

serves as an abrasive, causing both the chain and the cogs to wear more quickly. Clean chains and cogs shift better, too.

3. Once the cogs are clean, attend to the inner parts. Spin the cassette a few times. If you hear only the familiar sound of the ratcheting mechanism, proceed with lubrication. If you hear grinding sounds, as though there are little particles of sand partying inside, you should try to clean out the grit. It's usually possible to flush out foreign matter by dripping oil or some type of solvent through the mechanism. (Don't try to disassemble a cassette body. They aren't meant to be serviced.)

Look for a crack between the outer and inner cassette bodies by spinning the cassette and watching for where they are separated. Usually, you can find this without removing the cassette from the hub.

Drip bicycle oil or medium-weight motor oil into the mechanism, spinning the cassette to help the oil work its way around. Put a rag underneath to catch any excess that drains through. There's a handy tool available called the Morningstar Tools Freehub Buddy that allows you to flush and lubricate cassette bodies.

Step 4

4. If your cassette still feels gritty, try a penetrating oil-and-solvent mixture such as WD-40. Rotate the cassette while you spray the solvent mixture into it (see photo). Wipe away any excess, and lubricate the cassette once again with oil.

Some people use a more potent solvent, such as kerosene. If you do, you may have to oil your cassette several times before the lubricant is adequately replaced. A penetrating oil should be able to do the job.

Cassette Removal and Disassembly

1. To replace a broken spoke, change gear ratios, or replace worn cogs, it's necessary to remove the cassette from the hub. This is easy to do with the correct tools. For Shimano, SRAM, and Campagnolo cassettes, it requires one chainwhip, the appropriate cassette lockring remover, and a large adjustable wrench. For old cassettes (ones without lockrings), two chainwhips will do the trick.

Start disassembly by removing the rear wheel from the bike. If it's a modern cassette, you'll see a spline pattern at the center of the small cog; this accepts a special lockring remover.

2. Unscrew the quick-release mechanism, and insert the cassette lockring remover into the spline. For extra stability, reinstall the quick-release (remove the springs first) to hold the remover in place. This will prevent the tool from rocking and getting damaged when you apply force.

Step 2

3. Stand the wheel up (hold it or lean it against something), and wrap the chain section of a chainwhip around the largest cog, placing the handle forward (in the drive direction). Then place a large adjustable wrench on the flats of the lockring remover with the handle facing the other direction (see photo). Hold the chainwhip handle and push down on the adjustable wrench to loosen the lockring.

Step 3

113

Step 4

Step 5

4. Once it's loose, remove the quick-release and, still holding the chainwhip, unscrew the lockring completely, turning the remover by hand. Once the lockring is removed, the cogs will slide off the hub.

5. Some cassette gear clusters are assembled with bolts or screws (see photo) or are attached to a carrier, which you'll see when you remove the gear cluster. In order to separate the cogs on these, it's necessary to remove the hardware. Just be sure to keep everything in order as you remove it so you can reassemble the cassette correctly.

WATCH THIS FIX:

FIND A STEP-BY-STEP VIDEO OF HOW TO REPLACE A CASSETTE AT
www.bicycling.com/video/remove-and-install-cassette

CHAPTER 13

REAR DERAILLEUR

Caring for the important link that moves the chain across up to 11 gears

Today's rear derailleurs are strong and incredibly accurate, but they're still vulnerable to problems that are obvious (crashes) and not so obvious (dirt, corrosion, wear). Here's what you need to know to keep yours running—and shifting—just right.

WHAT'S IN THIS SECTION

- REAR DERAILLEUR BASICS
- REMOVE AND INSTALL A REAR DERAILLEUR
- ADJUST A REAR DERAILLEUR
- CHAIN ALERT!
- STRAIGHTEN A BENT HANGER
- TROUBLESHOOTING REAR DERAILLEURS

Rear Derailleur Basics

Anatomy of a Rear Derailleur

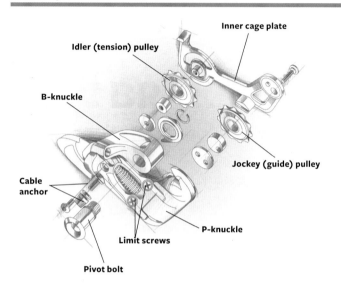

Inner cage plate

Idler (tension) pulley

B-knuckle

Jockey (guide) pulley

Cable anchor

P-knuckle

Limit screws

Pivot bolt

Short Cage versus Long Cage

Rear derailleurs made for double-chainring road bikes have short chain cages (bottom), while those made for wide-range, triple-chainring bikes—such as mountain bikes—have longer cages (top) for greater amounts of chain wrap.

Keep It Straight

The pulley cage ought to be parallel to the centerline of the bike. If it's straight when sighted from behind, an imaginary line drawn through the cassette cog will bisect the pulley wheels. If the cage tilts in toward the wheel, either the cage, the derailleur body, or the hanger (possibly even the dropout tab the hanger is attached to) may be bent.

Remove and Install a Rear Derailleur

1. The rear derailleur is positioned beneath the cassette and fastened by a bolt to a hanger, which sits beneath the right rear dropout. The dropouts are the slotted metal pieces that hold the rear wheel and are located at the junctions of the seatstays and chainstays.

2. The derailleur hanger on a high-quality bike is usually integrated into the right rear dropout (see photo). An integrated hanger contributes to better shifting by being stiffer than a bolt-on hanger. Some integrated hangers, such as the one shown here, feature replaceable sections that prevent major frame damage if you bend the derailleur badly.

Step 2

3. Before removing a rear derailleur for cleaning or replacement, you must free it from both the shift cable and the chain. To remove the cable, loosen the bolt that fastens it to the body of the derailleur and slip it out.

Freeing the chain from the derailleur can be done in one of two ways. One way is to use a chain tool to break a link in the chain, then pull one end of the chain free from the derailleur cage (see photo). Removing the chain makes sense if it needs cleaning or replacement.

4. The simpler method: Use a wrench to loosen the bolt that holds the idler pulley on the derailleur (see photo on page 120). Remove the idler pulley so the chain can

Step 4

be lifted off the jockey pulley. You may need to move the derailleur cage plates apart to free the chain. The derailleur can then be unbolted from the hanger and cleaned or replaced.

5. When installing a rear derailleur, follow the same procedure in reverse. Bolt it onto the hanger, then replace the chain and shift cable. Before tightening the cable, put the wheel back on the bike and make sure that the chain is positioned on the smallest cassette cog so the derailleur is free to move to its outer limit.

Operate the shift lever to make sure it's in its starting position so that the cable has all the available slack. Then thread the cable through the anchor on the derailleur body. Hold the cable taut with a pair of pliers and tighten the anchor bolt with a wrench.

6. After installing a new rear derailleur, check its range of motion and adjust it properly. Even if you are only remounting your old derailleur after a cleaning, it is a good idea to check the adjustment. Make sure the wheel is properly positioned on the frame before fine-tuning the derailleur.

WATCH THIS FIX:

FIND A STEP-BY-STEP VIDEO OF HOW TO INSTALL A REAR DERAILLEUR AT
www.bicycling.com/video/install-rear-derailleur

Adjust a Rear Derailleur

1. Place the bike in a repair stand. Check the derailleur adjustment by pedaling with your left hand while shifting with your right. Adjust the inner throw of your rear derailleur first. Shift the chain onto the largest cog. It should seat quickly on the cog. If it hesitates or goes into the spokes, adjust the derailleur with the low-gear adjusting screw. It's probably the upper one or the one nearest the rear (see photo). Counterclockwise turns allow the derailleur to move closer to the spokes. Clockwise turns limit travel.

Step 1

2. Shift the chain to the smallest cassette cog. Turn the high-gear adjusting screw until the pulleys line up beneath the small cog (see photo).

With your bike still mounted on the repair stand, spin the crankarms and run through the gears. Pay attention to the shifts onto the largest and smallest cogs (the ones you used to set the derailleur adjustments).

If there's any hesitation in these shifts or a lot of clatter after the shifts—or any sign that the chain might jump off the cogs—

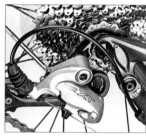

Step 2

fine-tune the adjustments until the shifts become quiet and accurate.

3. Some derailleurs have a third screw called the B-tension screw or the B-angle screw (see photo on page 122). This adjusts the clearance between the jockey pulley and the cogs.

Chain Alert!

After installing a new rear derailleur or changing the sizes of chainrings or cassette cogs, you may need to alter the chain length in order for the derailleur to shift properly. See page 106 for more.

Step 3

On single-pivot derailleurs like those manufactured by SRAM, the B-tension screw is used to directly adjust the distance between the jockey pulley and the largest cog. This distance should be about $\frac{1}{4}$ inch (6 millimeters)—close enough for quick shifting but clear enough that the chain can pass freely from the second-largest cog to the largest.

Double-pivot derailleurs rely on a spring inside the B-knuckle to actively adjust the cog–jockey clearance for each gear. The ideal setting can be a bit elusive. Adjust the B-tension screw so the pulley rides as close to the cogs as is practical without making noise in any gear.

Straighten a Bent Hanger

When a bike falls over or gets hit on its right side, the rear derailleur can be damaged. Fortunately, the most likely damage, a bent hanger, is not expensive

to repair—and you might be able to fix it yourself. If your derailleur-fastening bolt has a hex head, insert a wrench into it and use it and the derailleur body to lever the hanger back into line (see photo). Relying on the hex key alone may damage the derailleur pivot bolt or the key itself, so put a hand behind the derailleur and pull with it as you pull up on the bolt with your other hand. When you get home, perfect the "adjustment" with the aid of a derailleur hanger alignment tool.

4. Fine-tune the derailleur so it moves the chain to a new cog with each click of the shift lever. Do this with the adjustment barrel. Use your right hand to shift to the smallest cog while turning the crankarm with your left. Shift one click. The chain should instantly move to the second-smallest cog and stay there. If it doesn't, turn the barrel adjuster counterclockwise one-eighth of a turn and

Step 4

try again. Continue to turn the barrel until shifts are quick and precise. If you go too far, the system will run noisily. In that case, turn the barrel clockwise one-eighth of a turn at a time as you pedal until the noise stops.

As a final check, shift through all the gear combinations, making sure that the system works quickly and quietly.

WATCH THIS FIX:

FIND A STEP-BY-STEP VIDEO OF HOW TO ADJUST A REAR DERAILLEUR AT www.bicycling.com/video/adjust-rear-derailleur

Troubleshooting Rear Derailleurs

5 COMMON PROBLEMS, SOLVED!

PROBLEM: You shifted into the rear wheel and trashed the rear derailleur. How do you ride home?

SOLUTION: Separate the chain with your chain tool (you did bring one along, didn't you?), extract the chain from the derailleur, and rejoin the chain on the middle chainring and cassette cog. Pull the derailleur out of the spokes and limp home on your one-speed.

PROBLEM: You shift the lever, but the derailleur doesn't quite shift into gear and there are a lot of clicking noises as you pedal.

SOLUTION: The derailleur may be bent. Have it checked. If it's not bent, the cable tension has probably changed. If the shifting hesitates when moving to larger cogs, turn the adjusting barrel in one-eighth-turn increments toward the large cogs. If shifting to smaller cogs is the problem, turn the barrel toward them.

PROBLEM: You broke the shift cable and cannot shift into an easy gear to get home.

SOLUTION: If there's enough cable still attached to your derailleur, pull it (by hand) into a mid-range gear and secure the upper end of the shift cable beneath a bottle-cage screw. Now you can ride home with your bike in that gear.

PROBLEM: The rear derailleur makes a constant squeaking noise.

SOLUTION: The pulleys are dry and need lubrication. Try dripping some lube on the sides. If that doesn't work, disassemble the pulleys (one at a time), grease the bearing surfaces, and then reassemble.

PROBLEM: Shifting is difficult.

SOLUTION: The cables might be dirty. Shift onto the large cog, then move the shift lever back (without pedaling) to create cable slack. Lift the housings out of the stops, slide them down to expose the cable, oil or grease the cable, and reassemble the housings.

CHAPTER 14

HUBS

Adjustment, overhaul, and lubrication of the heart of your wheels

Most high-quality hubs need to be checked and adjusted only twice a year. Unsealed hubs need an overhaul at least every other year. Put in more than 3,000 miles a year? Overhaul annually. Ride a lot during particularly nasty weather? Overhaul! Rust can ruin bearings.

If you have sealed cartridge bearings, the above rules don't apply—you can go much longer between overhauls. That said, we've still got advice for you here.

Read on to learn how to keep your hubs spinning smoothly.

WHAT'S IN THIS SECTION

- HUB BASICS
- ADJUST CONE-AND-LOCKNUT HUBS
- IS THAT A CARTRIDGE BEARING?
- OVERHAUL CONE-AND-LOCKNUT HUBS
- OVERHAUL AND ADJUST A CAMPAGNOLO HUB EQUIPPED WITH AN OVERSIZE AXLE
- LUBRICATE SEALED CARTRIDGE BEARINGS
- TROUBLESHOOTING HUBS

Hub Basics

Anatomy of a Hub

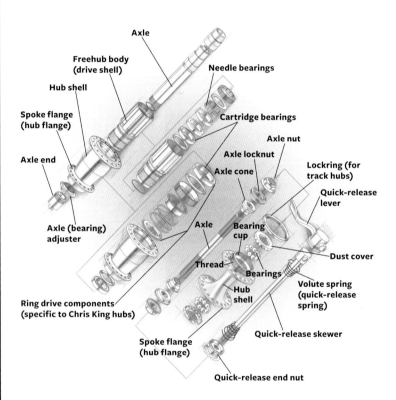

Axle

Freehub body
(drive shell)

Needle bearings

Hub shell

Spoke flange
(hub flange)

Cartridge bearings

Axle nut

Axle locknut

Lockring (for
track hubs)

Axle end

Axle cone

Quick-release
lever

Axle (bearing)
adjuster

Axle

Bearing
cup

Dust cover

Thread

Bearings

Hub
shell

Volute spring
(quick-release
spring)

Ring drive components
(specific to Chris King hubs)

Quick-release skewer

Spoke flange
(hub flange)

Quick-release end nut

Does Your Hub Need an Overhaul?

With the wheel off, grasp one end of the axle with the thumb and index finger of your dominant hand. Turn the axle slowly through a few revolutions. Does it feel rough and seem to catch in pits? If so, it's too tight or the hub is full of dirt or corrosion.

If your hub doesn't feel tight or gritty, check it for looseness. Wiggle the axle up and down and from side to side. If it moves in these directions, causing a slight knocking feeling, it's too loose.

Continuing to ride with the hub in any of these conditions will cause unnecessary wear and limit how well the bike can perform. Read on for how to adjust them perfectly.

Adjust Cone-and-Locknut Hubs

In a cone-and-locknut hub, ball bearings ride between a hardened steel cup fitted into the hub shell and a hardened steel cone threaded onto the axle. The adjustment is maintained by a locknut that threads against the cone so it doesn't spin out of place.

All cone-and-locknut hubs adjust in the same basic manner, though rear hubs might require a few additional steps.

1. Remove the wheel from the bike. Lay the wheel flat on a workbench. Remove the axle nuts or quick-release. Grab the axle with your fingers and turn it back and forth to see if it's too tight. Then move the axle back and forth to see if it's too

Is That a Cartridge Bearing?

If, after you've removed the locknut and cone, you see a flat plastic seal (see photo), your hub has cartridge bearings. The bearing assembly is a pre-manufactured unit and is fitted into the hub shell with the bearing adjustment preset. You may need to take these hubs to your local shop for maintenance. Consult your dealer before attempting to service them. Or turn to page 135 for info on how to lube the bearings.

loose. If the wheel has a quick-release mechanism, remember that it compresses things a bit—a hub that feels a little loose off the bike might feel okay on the bike. Remount the wheel, then check to see if the axle still seems loose.

Step 2

2. Before adjusting any hub, one set of cone and locknut must be locked in place on the axle. On front hubs, this can be done on either side, while on rear hubs, it should be done on the right (drive) side. Always check that this is tight. It will save you the frustration of an adjustment that won't keep.

First, remove the cassette (see page 113) to expose the right-side cone and locknut. Now remove the left-side locknut, lock washer, spacers (if there are any), and cone, and push the axle to the right to expose the right-side cone. (Be careful around the bearings. If you dislodge any, poke them back into place.)

3. With the axle pushed to the right, hold the cone with a wrench, grip the right locknut with another wrench, and tighten the two against each other to secure them in place.

Step 4

4. Push the axle back into the hub and screw on the left-side cone by hand until it rests against the bearings. Then add the spacers, lock washer, and locknut, and snug the pieces in place by turning the cone counterclockwise while turning the locknut clockwise with the wrenches. Twirl the axle between your fingers to check the adjustment. If it binds, the adjustment is too tight. Loosen it slightly by holding the right-side locknut with a wrench and the left-side cone with a cone wrench (see photo).

If the hub is too loose, hold the right-side locknut with a wrench while turning the left cone clockwise until the play disappears. Still holding the right locknut with a wrench, snug the left locknut against the left cone. Secure the left side by placing wrenches on the cone and locknut and tightening them against each other.

It may take a few tries to get a perfect adjustment. Keep at it. If it's difficult to make a good adjustment, the hub might be damaged or full of dirt. Time for an overhaul.

Overhaul Cone-and-Locknut Hubs

1. If your hub is equipped with a quick-release mechanism, thread the adjusting nut off the end of the quick-release skewer and pull the skewer out of the axle. Put the cone-shaped spring back on the skewer so you don't lose it, and then partially thread on the nut. Set the quick-release assembly aside before doing the hub overhaul.

Step 1

2. Hold the wheel vertically and remove the locknut, spacers, and cone from one side of the axle, keeping them in order. The axle can now be slid out the other side: Hold the wheel horizontally over a rag while removing the axle from the top to ensure that bearings don't bounce away if they fall out. Leave the cone and locknut on the other end of the axle in place to simplify hub reassembly. You'll automatically have the proper amount of axle on each side of your hub.

3. Remove the bearings from the cups and set them aside. They're a good initial indicator of the condition of the hub's bearing cups as well as the number and size of replacement bearings you'll need.

Spray a light solvent or degreaser into the cups, and wipe them clean with a rag. Rinse the cups with rubbing alcohol and let them air-dry. Visually inspect for pits, cracks, or irregular wear. Pitted cups on inexpensive hubs are a cue to replace the hubs or wheels altogether. Some higher-quality hubs can be saved by installing replacement cups. Check with your local shop about this solution.

Step 4

4. If there is a significant amount of dirt inside the hub, pry the dust seals out of the shell before cleaning. These seals are delicate, so proceed carefully. Gently pry at the cover from several angles using a flat-blade screwdriver. Once the covers are out, clean and inspect the cups and covers as described above.

Step 5

5. If you're replacing a Shimano freehub, this is the time to do it. Insert a 10-millimeter hex key inside the freehub body, and turn it counterclockwise to remove the retaining bolt. The retaining bolt may be very tight. You might want to clamp your hex key in a bench vise and use the wheel for leverage to ease removal.

Fit a new freehub body onto the hub shell's splines. Clean and grease the threads of the retaining bolt, and reinstall it in the freehub body and hub shell.

6. Clean the axle and roll it on a level surface. If it wobbles, it's bent and needs to be replaced. Take the axle to the bike shop to get the proper replacement.

If the cones are excessively worn and need to be replaced, you must remove the one still on the axle. Before loosening the locknut, measure and record the position of the cone on the axle so the new one can be threaded to the same location.

If all is well, use your cone wrenches to ensure that the cone and locknut are tight against one another.

7. Grease the axle well. If both cones came off the axle, put one of them back on and carefully thread it down to its proper position. Replace the lock washer and locknut, and lock the nut against the cone as previously explained.

8. Got all your parts? Time to reassemble the hub. Fit the dust seals back on the hub shell, seating them properly so the cones can be correctly adjusted. Some metal dust seals fit so loosely that they won't stay in place. An easy fix is to gently grip the edge with the jaws of a diagonal cutter, and pull it out very slightly. Repeat at two other spots so that there are three points, each about one-third of the way around the seal, that are slightly pulled out. The seal will be a tight fit and stay put.

Step 8

Apply a thick bead of fresh grease inside each of the bearing cups. Insert the correct number and size of new ball bearings into each side of the hub. Typically, a rear hub will hold nine $1/4$-inch bearings per side and a front will hold ten $3/16$-inch bearings per side. The grease will hold the bearings in place for the moment.

Slide the axle partway into the hub to secure the bearings in the cup. Insert the new bearings into the other cup. Once they are all in place, slide the axle completely through the hub.

Step 9

9. Thread the cone onto the axle until it makes contact with the bearings. Twirl the axle to seat the bearings, and then adjust the cone until there's no tightness or play in the hub.

10. When the adjustment is right, slide on the spacers in the correct order, followed by the locknut. Hold the adjustable cone with a cone wrench while you tighten the locknut against it. Slide the quick-release skewer back through the axle, and thread on its nut. Remount the wheel on the bike.

Overhaul and Adjust a Campagnolo Hub Equipped with an Oversize Axle

Campagnolo has devised a simple method for overhauling and adjusting its over-size-axle hubs. Note that the freehub body stays in place. This design uses cartridge bearings that don't require regular maintenance.

Step 1

1. Lay two rags or paper towels on your workbench (you'll need them later). Remove the quick-release skewer, and set it and its springs aside. If you have an older Campy wheel, the left side of the hub may have a pinch bolt on the adjusting ring; loosen it with a 2.5-millimeter hex key.

2. Remove the left-side axle cap using a pair of 5-millimeter hex keys, one in each

axle end. Turn them counterclockwise to
remove the axle cap. Keep track of the
thin washer that's between the axle cap
and axle.

3. The adjusting ring will now thread off
the axle. It may require a wrench to start.

4. Lightly tap the end of the axle with a
plastic or rubber hammer to free the axle
from the collet that holds the cone in
place. The axle is made of aluminum, so
don't use a metal hammer for this step.
Pull the axle out from the right side and
remove the collet and cone from the left.
On rear hubs, you may need to slowly
rotate the freehub body counterclockwise
as you pull it out, in order to let the
ratchet pawls snap free.

Step 2

Step 4

5. Carefully pry the white seals out of the
hub using a pick or small flat-blade screwdriver. Be gentle! Too much force can
deform the seals, rendering them unusable. Remove the bearings and retainers
from the hub shell. Pay attention to the orientation of the retainers in the hub;
you'll need to reinstall them facing the same way. You can discard the retainers if
you have a complete new set. If not, pop the old bearings out, clean the retainers
thoroughly with degreaser and then rubbing alcohol, and press new bearings into
place.

6. Clean everything. Do this first with degreaser and a rag. After degreasing, use
rubbing alcohol and a clean rag or paper towel to rinse everything. Lay all the
cleaned parts out onto a clean rag. Cover both cups in the hub shell with a bead of

Step 6

Step 7

Step 8

fresh grease; then put the bearing retainers in place with the retainers facing in and the exposed bearings facing out.

7. Press the seals back over the bearing retainers in their cups. They should pop easily into place. Slide the axle in from the right, then slip on the left-side cone and collet. On rear hubs, you may need to slowly rotate the freehub body counterclockwise to allow the ratchet pawls to slip into place. Thread the adjusting ring into position, but don't tighten it yet. Use two 5-millimeter hex keys to tighten the axle cap and washer back on the axle end.

8. Bearing adjustment of this system is independent of quick-release tension. Thread the adjusting ring down by hand until you feel the cone make contact with the bearings. Use an adjustable wrench to turn the adjusting ring down just a fraction of a turn to properly preload the bearings. Turn and wiggle the axle with your fingers. It should spin smoothly and not bind, with none of the looseness you want with conventional quick-release hubs. If your adjustment is too tight, back the adjusting ring off, and tap the axle end with a plastic hammer to release the collet's grip on the axle. Then start the adjustment again. When the adjustment feels right, tighten the pinch bolt on the adjusting ring.

9. Put the quick-release skewer back through the axle, and you're ready to roll.

Lubricate Sealed Cartridge Bearings

1. A cartridge bearing's seal protects the bearings, but it also allows moisture to be trapped inside, which is why it's important to regrease the bearings occasionally. To service this type of hub, first wipe off any dirt that has accumulated on the seal. Gently slide the tip of a sharp utility knife under the edge of the plastic seal, and pry the seal off the bearing cartridge (see photo). Be careful! Don't cut or bend the seal.

Step 1

2. Once you've removed the seal, you'll see the bearings beneath. Charge them with fresh grease by squeezing in enough to cover all the balls (see photo). Then simply press the seal back into place with your fingers until you feel it seat in the cartridge. Repeat for the other bearing, and reassemble the axle.

Step 2

To adjust bearings, screw in the cone until it rests against the bearing (or dust cap); snug the locknut against it; and, using two wrenches—one on the cone and another on the locknut—turn the parts against each other to lock the adjustment. When done, there should be no play in the axle, and the hub bearings should feel smooth and not tight when you turn the axle.

Some hubs employ clever axle designs that seem impossible to disassemble. It might take some detective work to find the secret, but if you can figure out how to get the hub apart, regreasing the bearings is easy. If it's a particularly challenging design, contact a shop or the manufacturer for advice.

> **WATCH THIS FIX:**
>
> **FIND A STEP-BY-STEP VIDEO OF SERVICING A CARTRIDGE BEARING AT** www.bicycling.com/video/servicing-cartridge-bearings

Troubleshooting Hubs

6 COMMON PROBLEMS, SOLVED!

PROBLEM: The wheel pulls out of the frame when you're climbing hills.
SOLUTION: Loosen the axle nuts or quick-release, center the wheel in the frame, and tighten the axle nuts or quick-release tighter than before.

PROBLEM: You clamp the quick-release, but it doesn't hold the wheel tight in the frame.
SOLUTION: The axle has to be the right length for the quick-release to work. Leave the wheel in the frame or fork and remove the quick-release. Look at the axle ends. Do they protrude past the outside faces of the dropouts? If so, remove the wheel, file the axle down until the ends are within the dropouts, and reattach the quick-release.

PROBLEM: You've reassembled the hub, and you can't get the adjustment right. It's either too tight or too loose.
SOLUTION: You may have put too many or too few bearings, or the wrong-size bearings, in the hub race. There are usually nine $1/4$-inch bearings in each side of the rear hub and ten $3/16$-inch bearings in each of the two front races.

PROBLEM: Your sealed cartridge bearing hub has developed lateral play that you feel when pushing sideways on the rim.
SOLUTION: A little lateral play is normal. A lot is a sign that the bearing cartridges may be worn. Replace them if possible, or have the hub checked by an expert or the manufacturer.

PROBLEM: It's harder than usual to close and open the quick-release.
SOLUTION: Remove the quick-release, and lubricate it with a penetrating oil. If this doesn't help, the quick-release may be worn out. Replace it.

PROBLEM: After a hub overhaul, the wheel won't sit straight in the bike.
SOLUTION: Make sure that the springs on the quick-release are installed correctly. The narrow end should always face in.

CHAPTER 15

WHEELS, RIMS, AND TIRES

How to care for tires, tubes, and rims

WHAT'S IN THIS SECTION

- WHEEL AND TIRE BASICS
- TIRE THREAD COUNTS, UNRAVELED
- PATCH A TUBE
- TIP FOR DISC BRAKE USERS
- PATCH A TUBELESS TIRE
- PATCH A TUBULAR TIRE
- REPLACE A BROKEN SPOKE
- TROUBLESHOOTING WHEELS AND TIRES

Well-built wheels don't need periodic maintenance apart from hub lubrication (unless they get damaged). And good-quality tires will last for many hundreds of miles if kept properly inflated and free of glass, metal, wire, and other debris. That said, it pays to be prepared. What follows can help you avoid costly repairs—and keep you rolling instead of wobbling down the road.

Wheel and Tire Basics

Anatomy of a Wheel

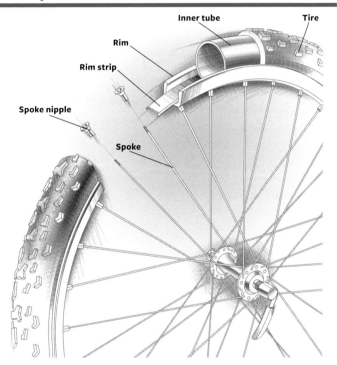

Inner tube

Tire

Rim

Rim strip

Spoke nipple

Spoke

Tire Thread Counts, Unraveled

Choosing a tire? Coarser casings (which means larger and fewer cords, of around 30 to 60 threads per inch, or TPI) usually result in a stiffer and more durable tire, while finer casings (100 TPI or more) yield a more supple, smoother-riding tire that can handle higher inflation pressure but may be less resistant to scuffs and cuts.

Know Your Valves

Schrader valves (*left*) are the same as those found on automobile tires; they require more force to inflate. Presta valves (*right*) are thinner, lighter, and easier to inflate.

WATCH THIS FIX:

FIND A STEP-BY-STEP VIDEO OF HOW TO INFLATE A TIRE AT
www.bicycling.com/video/inflate-bike-tire

Remove a Clincher Tire

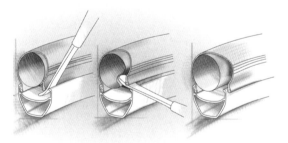

First, deflate the tube and push the tire bead toward the center trough of the rim, as shown above. Then use a tire lever to pry the bead over the side of the rim.

Install a Tubeless Tire

Tubeless and tubeless-ready tires rely on a special rim shape or rim strip to hold the tire bead in place and create an airtight seal.

WATCH THIS FIX:

FIND A STEP-BY-STEP VIDEO OF HOW TO INFLATE A TIRE AT
www.bicycling.com/video/install-tubeless-ready-tire

Patch a Tube

1. Remove the wheel from the bike. Mark the tire next to the valve stem to establish the relationship between the tire and tube (or simply always place the tire label by the valve stem). This makes it easier later to locate foreign matter that may still be embedded in the tire casing.

Tip for Disc Brake Users

Disc brakes can become very hot during a ride and are also very sensitive to oil contamination. The trace amounts of oil on your skin can sometimes be enough to ruin a pair of disc brake pads. To avoid unnecessary contact with the brake disc, mount your quick-release levers on the side opposite the disc.

Step 2

2. If any air remains in the tire, let it out by pressing on the valve (unscrew the tip of a Presta valve first). Start your tire removal on the side of the wheel opposite the valve to minimize the chances of damaging it. Squeeze the sides of the tire toward the trough at the center of the rim to produce slack, then hook a tire lever under the edge of the tire bead and pull it over the rim. (Use a good set of plastic tire levers with no sharp edges that could further damage the tube.) Hook the other end of the tire lever to a spoke.

Move a few inches along the rim, hook a second tire lever under the same bead, pull the bead over the rim (see photo), and hook the tire lever to a spoke. Once you get several inches of the tire bead over the rim edge, pull the rest of it over the rim by hand.

3. With one bead of the tire free from the rim, you can remove the tube for repair. There is no need to take the tire completely off the rim. Just push it over to one side while you remove the tube. Lift the tube's valve stem out of its rim hole, being careful not to damage it. Then slip the remainder of the tube out of the tire and pull it away from the rim.

Pump some air into the tube and try to pinpoint the puncture by listening or feeling for the escaping air. If a source of water is available (use a puddle on the trail or road), immerse the tube and watch for air bubbles. When you locate a repairable puncture, mark the tube at that point (dry it first if it's wet).

4. Pull the tire off the wheel and lay it down. Spread the tube over the tire so the two are in the same position as when they were together on the wheel. Line up the valve stem with the mark you previously made on the tire. Then check both the inside and outside of the tire casing at the point of puncture. Remove any offending objects.

5. If you can't find the puncture in the tube, check the valve stem. Tubes on underinflated tires can shift position, allowing the rim to cut into the side of the stem. If the stem is cracked or cut, you'll need to replace the tube.

6. Spread the tube on a flat surface. Use the piece of sandpaper or the metal scraper from the tube repair kit to roughen up the puncture area. Brush off any dust with your hand.

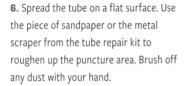

Step 6

7. Coat the roughened area of the tube with a fine, even layer of glue that's a little larger in diameter than the patch you intend to use. Make sure there are no globs that would prevent the patch from sealing properly. After spreading the glue on your tube, allow it to dry completely (this usually takes 5 minutes).

Step 7

8. Take a patch out of your repair kit. Choose a size that will cover the puncture and make good contact with the area all around it. Peel the foil from the sticky side of the patch, and fasten the patch in place on the tube.

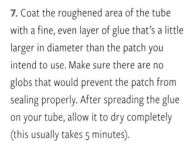

Step 8

9. To make sure you get a good seal, press down hard to force out any air bubbles. Inflate the tube enough to give it shape.

Push one bead of the tire back onto the rim, leaving the other bead and most of the casing hanging off the rim while you replace the tube. Temporarily push the second bead of the tire over the rim at the valve hole, and push it over the first bead to uncover the hole.

10. Fit the tube's valve stem through the hole, and pull the compressed section of the second tire bead back over the tube and off the rim. Starting in the area of the valve stem, work your way around the rim, tucking the tube back inside the tire.

Once the tube is in place, let the air out of it while you work the tire's second bead onto the rim. Begin at the stem. With the first few inches of the bead in place, push the valve stem up into the tire to ensure that no part of the tube around the stem is caught under the bead. Then continue your way around the rim.

11. Avoid using tire levers to put the tire on the rim, which could pinch the tube and damage it. In most cases, you should be able to do it with your hands alone. To get the slack you need for the final part of the process, go around the tire and squeeze the two beads together so they will drop down into the trough in the middle of the rim.

Step 12

12. When you get to the last section of tire, you may find it quite difficult to force it onto the rim.

Make sure you have given yourself all the available slack. Grasp the tire with both hands and, using a vigorous twisting motion of the wrists, try to roll the stubborn bit of bead over the edge of the rim. If this technique does not work, push the bead onto the rim bit by bit with your thumbs or the heels of your hands.

13. Once the tire is on the rim, push the valve up into the tire and pull it back down to be sure the stiff portion of the tube surrounding the valve is not trapped beneath the tire bead. Then work around each side of the rim, rolling the tire back

WATCH THIS FIX:

FIND A STEP-BY-STEP VIDEO OF FIXING A FLAT AT
www.bicycling.com/video/fix-flat-tire

and looking to see if the tube is trapped beneath the tire bead anywhere else. If it is, the tube will get pinched and the tire won't seat properly when you inflate it. Use a tire lever to poke the tube inside the tire. If everything looks okay, pump 20 to 30 pounds of pressure into the tube. If the stem is still straight and the tire is seating properly, continue pumping up to the recommended pressure (usually printed on the tire label).

Patch a Tubeless Tire

1. Tubeless tire service is remarkably similar to that for any other clincher. The first step is to remove the wheel from the bike. Deflate the tire completely, and pinch the sidewalls together firmly to get one of the tire beads to pop out of its channel. Then determine which bead has dislodged, and work your way around the wheel, pushing the rest of this bead into the center of the rim.

2. The rim's diameter is smallest at its center trough. With the bead in this position, you'll now have enough play in it to pull the tire up and away from the rim on one side, freeing the bead from the rim. Avoid the temptation to use tire levers except as a last resort. Using tire levers on a tubeless tire or rim can be damaging and render the system no longer airtight. If you must use tire levers, be extremely careful and use broad, flat plastic levers.

Step 3

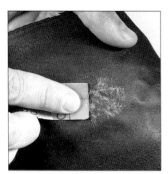

Step 5

Step 6

3. Push the second bead free of its channel in the same manner as you did the first. Once the second bead is dislodged and in the center of the rim, the tire should easily come off the rim.

4. Check the tire inside and out for the cause of the puncture, mark the location, and remove the foreign matter. If you're on the trail, the quickest way to get rolling again is to remove the valve stem from the rim and install a tube in the same manner as you would on any other clincher tire (see "Patch a Tube" on page 141). You can then patch the tire itself in the comfort of your home shop.

5. Back at the shop? Good. Turn the tire inside out at the point of the puncture, and scuff it heavily with the coarse sandpaper or rasp included in your patch kit. Scuff an area around the hole slightly larger than the patch you plan to use.

6. Apply a glob of glue and spread it around the roughened area. Let the glue set up for several minutes. You're ready for the next step when the glue becomes cloudy.

7. Remove the foil backing from the patch and firmly press the colored (usually orange) side of the patch into the glue. Keep constant pressure on the patch for 2 to 3 minutes, then carefully peel the clear plastic from the patch. Though it can be left in place, removing the film will help you be sure the patch is completely vulcanized to the tire's lining. If the edges of the patch peel up, spread a small amount of glue over the top of the patch and smooth the edges down from the middle outward.

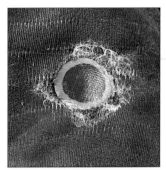

Step 7

8. While the patch dries, reinstall the valve stem and prepare the rim. Wipe the inside of the rim with a clean cloth to ensure a good seal with the tire. Spraying a diluted soap-and-water mixture (about 1/2 teaspoon of dish soap to 32 ounces of water) into the rim will make the tire's beads pop into their respective channels more easily and help maintain a good seal. If you don't have a spray bottle for this purpose, use a clean rag or sponge soaked in the same mixture.

Step 8

9. When the patch is dry, mount the tire. The first bead should slip into place easily. The starting point of the second bead is less important than with a tube-type tire, but it's slightly easier to start opposite the valve stem. Hold the wheel in your lap with the free bead facing up. Set the bead into the rim's center opposite the valve and work the bead over the rim wall little by little with your thumbs, moving them away from each other around the wheel.

As the last section of exposed bead becomes tight, recheck that the rest of the bead is settled into the center of the rim. Hold the wheel into your waist with the last section of bead away from you, and grip the tire firmly on both sides of the still-exposed section of bead. Roll your hands forward to stretch the last bit of bead over the rim. Some tires may prove difficult. Give it your absolute best shot to finish without using levers. Remember: There's no tube to pinch, but you don't want to compromise an expensive tubeless rim.

10. With the tire mounted, check once more that both beads are down in the rim's center. Tubeless systems require a quick burst of air to create the initial seal between tire and rim. Using a floor pump or compressed air, quickly pump the tire to about 20 psi (for mountain tubeless) or about 100 psi (for road tubeless). Once the initial seal is created, pump the tire steadily, listening for the beads to pop into place. When this begins, inspect the tire every few strokes until the bead is seated evenly all the way around the wheel. Once the tire has reached about 40 psi, you can help the process along by gripping the tire with the heel of your hand near a section that hasn't popped into place and pushing away with steady, even pressure. If necessary, keep inflating the tire up to (but not beyond) 60 psi for mountain bike tires and 120 psi for road tubeless. When the bead seat indicator (a textured line that extends about 1/16 to 1/8 inch beyond the rim wall) is fully and evenly exposed, that's it. Set the tire to your chosen riding pressure, reinstall the wheel, and go for a ride.

WATCH THIS FIX:

FIND A STEP-BY-STEP VIDEO OF HOW TO INSTALL A MOUNTAIN BIKE TUBELESS TIRE AT
www.bicycling.com/video/install-tubeless-ready-tire

Patch a Tubular Tire

1. When a tubular tire goes flat, stop riding on it immediately. Take the wheel off, and pump in a little air to try to locate the puncture while the tire is still on the rim. If you find the leak, mark the spot and proceed with the removal of the tire from the rim. If not, you'll have to pull the tire off the rim first.

If the tire was glued on properly, it won't come off the rim easily. Try gripping one section of the tire with both hands and rolling it over the side of the rim, pushing on its underside with your thumbs or palms. Once you get a section loose, it will be easier to get a good grip for pulling the rest of the tire off the rim.

If you weren't able to find the puncture while the tire was on the rim, pump some air back into the tire and hold it near your ear to listen for a leak. Even if you can't hear anything, you may be able to feel the escaping air hitting your face.

2. If you couldn't locate the puncture, immerse the tire in a pan of water and watch for escaping air bubbles. Once you see, hear, or feel escaping air, search for evidence of a puncture in the tire. Until you actually locate a cut or puncture, you can't be certain where the problem lies, because air can travel out of a hole in the tube and move several inches inside the tire before emerging.

Step 2

The most foolproof way of isolating a leak is to clamp off a small section of tire and pump air into the tire. If air escapes from the tire, loosen the clamp and move it along to another section. When no air escapes from the unclamped part, you know the problem lies within the clamped section. Take off the clamp and inspect that section to discover the source of the leak. Make clamps using a couple of pieces of two-by-four. Tighten them around the tire using a large C-clamp or the jaws of a vise (see photo).

3. The smaller the pieces of wood used, the more frequently you'll have to reposition them but the more narrowly you can pinpoint the source of the leak. It's

Step 3

important to know precisely where the tube needs repair before cutting the stitching. because you want to minimize how much you need to cut (and later restitch).

Once you've located the puncture, lift up a few inches of base tape in that area (see photo). The base tape covers the tire's stitches and is bonded to the tire with latex glue. This is a different glue than the type used to mount the tire to the rim. When the stitching is exposed, make a distinct mark across the seam to help you line up the edges of the tire for later restitching.

Step 4

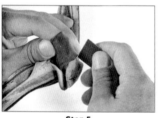

Step 5

Step 6

4. Use a sharp knife, razor blade, or (best of all) sewing seam ripper to cut enough stitches to allow you to pull out the section of tube needing repair.

5. Pull out that section of tube and roughen the punctured area with fine sandpaper. Spread a layer of patch glue over the area, and let it dry completely. (It'll lose its glossy appearance, usually after about 5 minutes.)

6. Find a patch of the appropriate size, and peel the protective backing from its sticky side. In order to get a good seal, place one edge of the patch on the tube first, and roll the remainder of the patch over.

7. Sprinkle a bit of talc over the patched area to prevent the tube from sticking to the tire. Check both inside and outside the tire to locate and remove any remaining foreign material that may repuncture

the tube once it's inflated and back in use. If any threads of the tire casing have
been severed, cut a piece of strong canvas, nylon, or old tire casing, and insert it
inside the casing over the damaged area. When the repaired tube is inflated, it'll
hold the patch in place. Push the tube back into place inside the tire. Straighten
the inner tape over the tube, and pull the edges of the casing together, lining up
the two halves of your mark.

8. Restitch the tire using the original
holes. (Creating new holes will weaken
the casing.) Be sure to begin by overlapping the old thread for several holes on
both sides of the repair area. If you're a
talented sewer, you may want to try to
duplicate the original thread pattern in
the tire. However, a simple overhand
stitch will work adequately (see photo).

Step 8

Tubular-tire repair kits provide thread, but any strong thread should work. Some
people prefer dental floss to the type of thread found in most kits. Just tie a
small knot in the end of your thread as if you were sewing on a button, and tie
off the other end when you complete the stitching. Fasten the base tape with
liquid latex.

9. Carefully scrape dried old glue off your rim as well as you can (you needn't get
it all off). If it's a new rim, sand it lightly with emery cloth, clean it with acetone or
alcohol, and add a layer of glue. If you've never put a tubular tire onto a rim before,
you may want to practice putting it on without glue first. Here's how. (Or skip to
step 11 for gluing tips.) Set the rim down on a clean floor with the valve hole at the
top. Insert the valve through the hole, and beginning at that point, stretch the tire
around the rim, working in both directions at once.

10. When you get to the last, difficult section, lift the rim off the floor and simultaneously stretch and roll the final part of the tire over and onto the rim (see photo).

Step 10

Work your way around the rim, checking to make sure the tire is on straight. When it looks right, inflate it. If the tire was difficult to get on, let it sit for a while, perhaps overnight, to let it stretch a little. Then deflate the tire and remove it from the rim for gluing.

11. Apply a dab of tubular cement between each spoke hole on the rim. Then run a bead of glue all the way around the rim. Apply a lighter coat to the base tape of the tire.

Step 12

12. Put a small plastic bag or a piece of plastic over your fingers and spread the glue around. After an hour, apply a second coat of glue in the same way.

When the second coat is tacky, proceed with the tire mounting. When you set the rim down, be sure the floor is clean, because you don't want to contaminate the glue (or floor).

Roll the tire onto the rim as you did before. Then spin the wheel and sight the tread to make sure the tire is on straight and that it's properly centered. If necessary, work it straight with your hands. Partially inflate the tire and put it onto your bike. If everything looks fine, inflate the tire to full pressure and let it sit overnight before using it.

Replace a Broken Spoke

1. Spokes don't demand a lot of maintenance. Primarily, your job is to make certain they're properly tensioned. Periodically work your way around each wheel, plucking each spoke to make sure that it's not loose. You'll spot a loose spoke both by the way it feels and by the way it sounds when plucked.

Use a spoke wrench to bring a loose spoke up to a level of tension that is similar to that of its neighbors. After you've tightened the loose spokes, check the wheel for trueness, and make further adjustments as needed.

Wheel truing is made easier and more precise when it's done in a truing stand. If you don't have access to such a stand, use your brake calipers to help you check your wheel, or rest a thumb on a brake pad and sight the gap between the rim and your thumbnail. Sighting between the brake pads or your thumb and the rim will allow you to see whether the wheel needs side-to-side truing (this can also help you determine if the wheel is out of round).

2. When a spoke breaks, it's best not to ride any farther on the wheel. Instead, push your bike to a place where it's safe to replace the spoke. If you must ride the bike, first weave the loose spoke end around an adjacent spoke, then ride slowly to your destination.

Replace the spoke with one of the same size. If you need a new nipple, roll the tire back, lift up the rubber strip that covers the tops of the nipples (called a rim strip), and take out the old nipple. Drop a new one in its place. Remove the broken spoke, and run the new one through the hub flange in the same direction as the old one.

Step 2

3. Pull your new spoke through the flange until its curved end is seated, then weave it through the other spokes, following the pattern of the old one. If in doubt, follow the pattern of the second spoke on either side of it.

Step 3

4. Before threading the new spoke into its nipple, apply a small amount of oil to its threads. This will make it easier to thread the spoke into the nipple and will help prevent it from freezing in the nipple over time. Then thread it on and use a spoke wrench to bring it up to tension.

When working on spokes, it's important to use the correct-size wrench. If the wrench flats on a nipple get rounded off, you'll have a difficult time adjusting that spoke. Also, before adjusting any of the old spokes, it's a good idea to spray a little penetrating oil at the points where the spoke enters the nipple and the nipple enters the rim. Rotate the wheel so that the oil will flow down into the threads after you spray it on.

Troubleshooting Wheels and Tires

13 COMMON PROBLEMS, SOLVED!

PROBLEM: Every time you fix a flat, the tire goes flat again.
SOLUTION: Check the tube carefully. Are the holes in one area? If they're on the bottom, the rim strip may be out of position, allowing the tube to get cut by the spokes. If they're on top, there may be some small sharp object still stuck in the tire. Find it by running a rag around the inside of the tire, and get it out of the tire. There might also be another hole: Remove the tube, inflate it, and hold it underwater. Any bubbles will lead you to a hole.

PROBLEM: You keep getting pinch flats.
SOLUTION: Put more air in your tires, or install wider tires.

PROBLEM: It's hard to install the tires because the tube gets in the way.
SOLUTION: Tire installation is easiest if you use a tube that's narrower than the tire. Switch to either narrower tubes or wider tires.

PROBLEM: You got the tire on but it won't sit right on the rim.
SOLUTION: Let the air out, wiggle the bad spot around, reinflate to about 30 psi, and roll the bad spot into place with your hands. Then inflate fully. If this doesn't

work, try letting the air out, applying a soapy solution to the tire along the bead, and reinflating.

PROBLEM: The patch won't stick to the tube.
SOLUTION: Put on enough glue and let it dry completely (about 5 minutes). Never touch the sticky side of the patch with your fingers. Don't blow on the glue to get it to dry faster, because you may get water on the glue.

PROBLEM: You can't get air in the tubes on your aero/deep-rimmed wheels.
SOLUTION: Get tubes with long enough valves (they must protrude enough to get the pump on), or get valve extenders. Be sure to leave the Presta valve unscrewed when you're installing the valve extenders.

PROBLEM: Your tubeless tire loses air slowly.
SOLUTION: Remove the tire and check the rim for foreign matter in the bead channel. A dent or nick in the rim can also cause slow air loss. Aside from rebuilding with a new rim, there is no way to repair this. If the rim is still able to hold a tire, you can use a standard tire and tube on a tubeless rim.

PROBLEM: You finish repairing a tubular tire and find that you've created an S shape in the tread.
SOLUTION: You stitched the tire up using the wrong holes. Cut your stitches and try again. Next time, mark the casing so you'll know which holes to use when restitching.

PROBLEM: You keep breaking spokes.
SOLUTION: Usually this is because the wheel was built with poor-quality spokes. Replace them with better-quality spokes, such as DT Swiss or Wheelsmith stainless steel models.

PROBLEM: It's always a struggle to install the wheel after removal. The wheel doesn't seem to want to fit into the frame.
SOLUTION: Remember to place the chain on the same cog it was on when you took the wheel off (usually the smallest cog). If you're doing that and it's still difficult, the frame dropouts may be bent, which can make wheel installation a pain. Have a shop check and align them with special tools.

PROBLEM: The wheels won't stay true.
SOLUTION: True them and make sure that the spoke tension is sufficient and uniform. If the spokes continually loosen, add a round of tension to the spokes, which should stabilize the wheel.

PROBLEM: There's a creaking sound from the wheels.
SOLUTION: The spokes may have loosened. Tighten them slightly. If they're tight, the spokes may be moving slightly at the cross, causing the sound. Lubricate each cross of the spokes with light oil, and wipe off the excess.

PROBLEM: The spokes on your radial-spoked wheel (on which the spokes travel directly from the hub to the rim without crossing other spokes) continually loosen.
SOLUTION: Try adding tension to the spokes. If the spokes loosen again, it's probably because of the spoke pattern. Radial spokes take shocks more directly than spokes that cross others, so they're more apt to loosen. To keep them tight, loosen all the nipples, apply a light thread adhesive to the nipples, and retension the wheel. Your loosening troubles should cease.

RESOURCES

Proper repair means having the right tools for the job. And not every job requires every tool. Here, we help you set up toolkits for various scenarios, from home to trail, and also give you a basic schedule for preventive maintenance. The rest is up to you!

The Bring-on-Your-Bike Tool Kit

Carry these with you when you ride, either in a bag under your seat or in a backpack.

- Spare tube (even if you use tubeless tires)
- Tube patch kit (contains patches, glue, and sandpaper; check the glue frequently, since it tends to dry out once opened)
- Tire boots (patches to repair cuts in the tire; a dollar bill or energy bar wrapper works in a pinch)
- Tire levers
- All-in-one mini tool, such as the Crank Brothers Multi 17 (a small tool that includes 2-, 2.5-, 3-, 4-, 5-, 6-, and 8-millimeter hex keys; a chain tool; a flat-blade screwdriver; a Phillips screwdriver; a T-25 Torx key; spoke wrenches; and 8- and 10-millimeter open wrenches). (See more on page 158.)
- Mini pump or frame pump (for your type of valve) or CO_2 cartridges and inflator
- Small length of wire (handy for making temporary "get home" repairs)
- Emergency money
- Cell phone
- Identification (written inside your helmet, too)

Multi-Tool Options

Multi-tools come in many configurations; choose one that matches your bike's small parts, and you could be saved from walking home.

Tools for the Home Workshop

The "Good" assortment outlined here is enough for most basic home repairs and then some. The "Ultimate" assortment is for if (or when) you get really serious. If you're new to maintenance, start small and add to your tool collection as you go. Buy high-quality tools as you need them, and eventually you'll have most of the items on this list.

Good Tool Assortment

GENERAL TOOLS	BICYCLE TOOLS
• Phillips screwdrivers (#1 and #2)	• Floor pump with gauge
• Flat-blade screwdrivers (7/32, 1/4, and 5/16 inch)	• Repair stand
• Standard pliers	• Tire levers
• Water pump pliers (e.g., Channellock)	• Pedal wrench
• Needle-nose pliers	• Cone wrenches (13 to 19 millimeters for adjusting wheel axle bearings)
• Small and medium locking pliers (e.g., Vise-Grip)	• Schrader valve core remover (to fix slow leaks in car-type valves)
• Diagonal cutter	• Cable cutter (to cut brake and shift cables without fraying)
• Hex keys (2, 2.5, 3, 4, 5, 6, 8, and 10 millimeters)	• Cable stretcher (aka "fourth hand," for adjusting brake cables)
• Torx keys (T-7, T-25, and T-40)	• Chain-tool/chain-rivet extractor (for removing, installing, and repairing chains)
• Metric combination wrench set (6 through 17 millimeters)	• Cassette lockring remover or freewheel remover that fits the cogset on your wheels
• Adjustable wrenches (8 and 12 inches)	• Chainwhip (for holding cassettes steady during lockring removal, or a pair to disassemble freewheels)
• 8-ounce ball-peen hammer	• Spoke wrench that fits your spoke nipples
• Plastic, rubber, or leather mallet	• Crankarm bolt wrench or 14-millimeter socket and ratchet handle
• Scissors	• Crankarm remover
• Tape measure (centimeters and inches)	• Chainring bolt spanner
• Hacksaw frame and blades (18 and 32 TPI, plus carbide blades for carbon fiber)	• Bottom bracket tool that fits your bottom bracket
• Utility knife	• Headset wrenches (if you have a threaded headset)
• Awl	• Suspension pump (if you have air-sprung shocks)
• Cold chisels (for cutting or carving metal)	
• Punches (for driving out or aligning things)	
• Outside calipers	
• Small magnet (useful for extracting ball bearings)	
• Rubber gloves	
• Safety glasses or goggles	

Ultimate Tool Assortment

Includes all the tools in the Good Tool Assortment plus:

- *Sutherland's Handbook for Bicycle Mechanics* (the definitive source for component measurements)
- Stainless steel ruler (6 inches/15 centimeters)
- Sturdy bench vise
- Solvent tank (a safe place to clean parts and store solvent)
- Truing stand
- Vernier caliper (for checking component dimensions)
- Dishing gauge (for centering the rim over the axle when building or truing wheels)
- Taps (for repairing threads; 5 millimeters $\times$ 0.8, 6 millimeters $\times$ 1.0, 7 millimeters $\times$ 1.0, 8 millimeters $\times$ 1.0, and 10 millimeter $\times$ 1.0)
- Tap handle
- Spoke tensiometer (for measuring spoke tension)
- Dropout alignment tools (for repairing bent dropouts)
- Thread pitch gauge (for measuring threads)
- Headset installation tools (bearing cup press, crown race tools, etc.)
- Spoke ruler
- Derailleur hanger alignment tool (for repairing bent hangers)
- Tapered reamer (for enlarging holes by hand)
- Rear triangle alignment indicator bar (for checking frame alignment)
- Round, half-round, and flat files in medium and coarse (for machining metal parts by hand)
- Electric drill and drill bits
- Bondhus hex keys (hex keys with ball-shaped ends ideal for working in tight spaces; 2, 2.5, 3, 4, 5, 6, 8, and 10 millimeters)
- Inside caliper
- Torque wrench
- Grinder with wire wheel
- Hex key bits (to fit torque wrench; 4, 5, 6, and 8 millimeters)

- Air compressor with blower attachment (to simplify tire inflation and grip installation)
- Snap ring pliers
- Lockwire pliers and lockwire (for securing disc brake hardware and wiring mountain bike grips in place)
- Tubing cutter
- Hydraulic disc brake bleed kit

Travel-Friendly Kits

Park Tool and Pedro's sell a variety of toolkits already assembled to meet the needs of mechanics who are jump-starting their tool collections. The kits range from basic starter kits to full-blown workbench-in-a-box options. Check them out at www.parktool.com and www.pedros.com.

Maintenance Schedule: Every Ride

BEFORE EVERY RIDE	AFTER EVERY RIDE	EVERY MONTH (MORE OFTEN IF RIDING 5 OR MORE DAYS PER WEEK)
Check the tire pressure.	Brush foreign objects off the tread and check the overall condition of the tires.	Wipe down the entire bike with a wet rag.
Make sure the chain is properly lubricated. See more on page 64.	Wipe or hose down the bike if it's very dirty. Be careful not to direct water at bearings or other sensitive components; bounce the bike to shake off the excess water, then store it in a warm, dry place.	Check for cracks or signs of stress on the frame, rims, crankset, fork, handlebar, and stem.
Make sure the brakes grab firmly. Make sure the wheels are centered in the frame and that the quick releases are firmly closed. See more on page 29.	Dry off the saddle if it's wet.	Hold the front wheel between your knees and try to turn the handlebar with one hand; if it moves easily, tighten the stem bolt(s).
Check that the brakes are properly aligned and the pads are in good condition. See more on page 70.	If the chain got wet, wipe it down and apply some fresh chain lube.	Give the chain, cogs, and chainrings a quick degreasing on the bike, and relubricate the chain. See more on page 104.
Check hydraulic brake lines for kinks or splits. See more on page 56.	After a wet ride, remove the seatpost, turn the bike upside down, and let the seat tube drain. Apply fresh grease or anti-seize compound before reinstalling the post (unless you have a carbon fiber frame or seatpost, in which case you should use assembly compound—a paste formulated to work with carbon and composite materials). See more on page 20.	Lubricate the bushings of the idler and jockey pulleys on the rear derailleur. See more on page 117.
Bounce the bike to detect rattles that might indicate loose or misadjusted parts.		Lubricate the pivot points on the front and rear derailleurs. See more on pages 76 and 117.
Check that you have your pump/inflator and your complete repair kit with you.		Check the crank bolts and chainring bolts for tightness. See more on page 85.
Lubricate the springs and pivot points on clipless pedals. See more on page 10.	Check hydraulic brake lines for kinks or splits. See more on page 56.	Overhaul the hubs. See more on page 126.
	Check the bearing adjustment on the front and rear hubs. See more on page 127.	Check that all the brake hardware is secure.

to Every Month

EVERY MONTH (CONTINUED)	EVERY 6 MONTHS	EVERY YEAR
Check the spoke tension and trueness of the wheels and adjust as needed. See more on page 152.	Check the adjustment on pedal bearings. See more on page 10.	Overhaul the headset. See more on page 7.
Check cables for kinks and fraying.	Check the bottom bracket for proper adjustment. See more on page 86.	Replace the cables and housings. See more on page 64.
Measure the chain and check the cogs and chainrings for excessive wear; replace if necessary. See more on page 97.	Check the seat tube for rust on steel frames.	Replace worn parts such as tires and brake pads.
Check the condition of the brake pads; replace if excessively or unevenly worn. For rubber rim-brake pads, pick out debris with an awl and remove glazing by scuffing with a half-round file.	Clean the cables and flush the cable housings with a light aerosol solvent.	Replace grips or handlebar tape. See more on page 29.
Clean the rims with rubbing alcohol.	Check all the hardware on the bike.	
Check accessory hardware (racks, bottle cages, etc.) for tightness.		
Check the condition of the glue on tubular (sew-up) tires.		
Clean and treat leather saddles with saddle soap or leather dressing.		
Check the headset for proper adjustment. See more on page 7.		
Check the rear suspension pivot bolts for proper torque.		

WATCH THIS FIX:

FIND A STEP-BY-STEP VIDEO OF A PRERIDE CHECK AT
www.bicycling.com/video/pre-ride-safety-check

Recommended Lubricants

PART	LUBRICANT
• Ball bearings	• Medium-weight bike grease
• Bottom bracket spindle	• Medium-weight bike grease (do not lubricate square-taper spindles unless directed to by the crankarm manufacturer)
• Brake cable	• Aerosol solvent to flush housing; if desired, lubricate using a lightweight oil
• Brake pivot	• Medium-weight bike grease or Teflon-based oil
• Brake spring	• Medium-weight bike grease
• Chain	• Chain lubricant of your choice; there are lots out there for different conditions
• Derailleur pivots	• Teflon-based oil
• Internal gear hubs	• Lightweight machine oil with no particulate additives
• Seatpost (steel or aluminum frame and/or seatpost)	• Medium-weight bike grease
• Seatpost (carbon fiber frame with any material seatpost; carbon fiber seatpost with any material frame)	• Assembly compound (a suspension of microscopic plastic beads in a nonpetroleum grease that enhances grip between clamped parts without affecting the carbon or resin)
• Seatposts (titanium frame with steel, aluminum, or titanium seatpost; titanium seatpost with steel, aluminum, or titanium frame)	• Anti-seize compound
• Stem (quill type)	• Medium-weight bike grease; substitute anti-seize compound if any titanium component is involved
• Stem (threadless type)	• Nothing
• Threads	• White lithium grease, medium-weight bike grease, anti-seize compound, or threadlocking compound, depending on the application

INDEX

Boldface page references indicate photographs. <u>Underscored</u> references indicate boxed text.